Praise for
HAPPY & STRONG

"Packed with wisdom needed now more than ever, this book lays out proven strategies that are bound to change countless lives. Use it to help you navigate a path to your own Happy & Strong."
—**JOHN C. MAXWELL,** #1 *New York Times*
bestselling author, coach, and speaker

"Jaime Villalovos is the real deal, which is rare. She is a great example of how to MAX OUT every area of your life and proof that you can have it all. You will feel that as you read this book. This is a must-read for all entrepreneurs."
—**ED MYLETT,** peak performance expert,
global keynote speaker, and bestselling author

"Jaime Villalovos is a unique woman who has been able to come out of an incredibly difficult childhood with a positive passion and a vision for a better life. With grit and determination to reach for her dreams, she has become a powerful advocate of balancing a strong family with meaningful work. Get ready to be inspired!"
—**LINDA EYRE,** #1 *New York Times* bestselling author,
international speaker, and expert on parenting,
life balance, and family strengthening

"Jaime is a principle-driven leader. After reading her engaging new book *Happy & Strong*, you will not only walk away inspired, but with so many tools to add more joy and balance to your life."
—**SEAN COVEY,** *New York Times* bestselling author
and president of FranklinCovey Education

"This is the story of a gritty, tough-as-nails little girl from a trailer in Montana who envisioned her ideal world and conquered it. Jaime Villalovos is living the American Dream, and this book is her blueprint for success."

—STEVE SIEBOLD, author of *177 Mental Toughness Secrets of the World Class*

"This book is for any driven woman who wants it all and is ready to define exactly what that means for her own life!"

—JENNA KUTCHER, host of the top-rated *Goal Digger* podcast, author, and educator

"If you care deeply about your long-term happiness and success, then put this book on your required reading list. You will be inspired as you learn sensible ways to help you achieve your vision and goals. Jaime's sincere and heartfelt advice, garnered from her hard-won life experience, will guide you there."

—JOHN ASSARAF, entrepreneur and bestselling author of *Having It All* and *The Answer*

"Winning and accolades mean nothing if your family doesn't come first. Having a book like *Happy & Strong* would have been great as we fine-tuned the balance and communication in our marriage and with our kids over the last couple of decades."

—SHANE AND LISA DORIAN, big wave pro surfing legend, inventor, coach, entrepreneurs, and owners of Kimi & Li Bikini Company

"Jaime is such an incredible example of a focused businesswoman, leader, and coach. I'm most impressed, however, by her personal life. She is the 'balanced life' queen!"

—**PENNEY OOI**, executive chairwoman for World Financial Group, philanthropist, entrepreneur, and mother

"For the two decades I've known Jaime, I can say without a shadow of a doubt that she walks her talk. This book is a must-read for everyone who wants to have the gift of mental and physical fortitude, as well as joy and fulfillment! *Happy & Strong* is more than a title to a book; it should be a goal for everyone to shoot for in their lives."

—**JEFF LEVITAN**, entrepreneur, philanthropist, and founder of All For One Foundation

"Jaime is nothing short of amazing! This is a true-life rags-to-riches story. No one is better at teaching how to win in *every* area of life than she. I'm so excited the world will have this book."

—**SIR JOHN SHIN**, executive producer of *Think and Grow Rich: The Legacy*, author of *How Rich Asians Think*, and serial entrepreneur

"In a world where people seem more and more willing to give up their personal sovereignty, this book will help you to recapture it. Jaime's story proves that anyone can do it if they're willing to do the work, and she gives tangible tools and tips to help you be happier in every area of your life."

—**RYAN MICHLER**, bestselling author, podcaster, and founder of Order of Man

HAPPY & STRONG

Create your dream life while enjoying the journey

JAIME M. VILLALOVOS

Foreword by Ed Mylett

Forefront
BOOKS

Published by Forefront Books.

ISBN: 978-1-63763-082-2 (Print)
ISBN: 978-1-63763-083-9 (eBook)

Cover Design by Mercedes Piñera
Interior Design by Bill Kersey, KerseyGraphics

To Shawn,
My best friend and partner for time and all eternity.

CONTENTS

FOREWORD

In the twenty years I have known Jaime, I have seen many versions of her. This is true for most long-term relationships, but with Jaime, it's been different. I've had the pleasure of watching her evolve from an aggressive, hard-charging, extremely focused, motivated young and single entrepreneur in her early twenties to a graceful, powerful, intuitive leader, wife, mother, and friend.

Now don't get me wrong. Everybody changes and grows! The difference with Jaime is *how* she has changed and grown. Most people become a different or new version of themselves, often leaving behind strengths in the process, sometimes even a wave of destruction. Jaime has figured out a way to become a better version of herself each time she has grown, while expanding her strengths. She is still aggressive, hard-charging, extremely focused, and motivated. This has helped her to rise to the top 1 percent of the 1 percent in income, wealth, and business. This in itself has been impressive to me, but in my opinion, it's her least impressive accolade.

What has impressed me the most about Jaime is the life she has built with her husband, Shawn; the impact it has had on hundreds of thousands of lives; and the foundation it has been built on.

In a world where it has become easier to become fiscally wealthy, it is harder to find people, men and women alike, who can navigate the balancing act of growing a successful business, nurturing a thriving marriage, showing up as a parent, and staying *happy and strong*, unflinching in their principles and faith. Jaime is a great example of how to "MAX OUT" every area of your life. Her book is a must-read for all entrepreneurs.

This is where I think Jaime can help *you*. Her concept of "happy and strong" is not new. We all want to be happy and strong—physically, emotionally, financially. Our biggest challenge, though, is that most people don't have the tools to achieve it.

This book will not only inspire you but also give you tangible tools to achieve your version of "Happy & Strong." If you want more success financially, Jaime can help you. If you want to be healthier physically, she can help you. If you want to be a better wife or husband, she can help you. If you want to be a better mother or father—you get the point.

The only prerequisite is that *you* have to be willing to put in the work. This book is worth your time. More than that, it's worth your effort. I'm excited that Jaime is making her strategies public, and more excited to see it positively impact *your* life.

Jaime Villalovos is the real deal, which is rare. She is proof that you can "have it all." You will feel that as you read this book.

I am grateful to have helped play a part in her success and to watch her growth this last twenty-plus years. I am grateful for her example. Kristianna and I are most grateful for her friendship and how it has enhanced our lives.

Within its pages, this book has tools to enhance your life. I pray that you use them well.

God bless,
Ed Mylett

INTRODUCTION

To tell you the truth, I never planned to write this book. I just kept having this nagging feeling that I needed to. That maybe *you* needed me to. Because I still remember what it was like when I was struggling to make my goals a reality (actually, I was struggling just to pay the bills). In debt, in a little apartment, eating ramen noodles, and just trying to get by. I wish this book had existed for *me* back then.

The goal of *Happy & Strong* is not only to help give you a path to the success you want in your life but to make sure you find joy along the way and feel fulfilled when you finally arrive. After all, financial and business success without fulfillment is still failure.

I see so many amazing people give up on their dream life because "having it all" seems impossible. Or they reach financial success but are still unhappy and stressed. To me, being Happy & Strong means you achieve everything you desire in business, in your family life, spiritual life, fitness, and wellness. It means you win, are fulfilled, and have no regrets! I've been able to build an amazing life that so many can only dream of, and now nothing makes me happier than helping others do the same. Wouldn't it be great to live a life you absolutely adore instead of one where you constantly feel pressure, worry, and unfulfilled?

This book is designed to help you achieve *your* idea of success. I've been on both sides of the spectrum, from growing up very poor to now being in the top 1 percent of 1 percent (0.01 percent) of income earners in the world. Having money is way more fun. But along the way, I've battled with wondering if the price I was paying for success was too high.

When I started out in business, I was a young, single woman with big dreams and tons of tenacity. Then I had to adjust to having a partner in business when I got married. Once we had kids, again, I had to adapt to continue to grow. I battled with the nagging distraction in my mind, "Am I doing what's right for my family? Am I doing what's right for me? Is it OK that I want more? Is it selfish to keep chasing new, bigger dreams?"

There will be challenges and sacrifices for sure, but what exactly is the price tag for success? That's been the question so many ambitious champions like yourself have wondered. As ambitious as I am, I made up my mind a long time ago that if the price for success is my family or my happiness, then that price is too high. Who cares if you have millions of dollars but you end up divorced or your kids are screwed up and don't want to talk to you?

I have a good friend named Rusty who didn't want to pay that price either. Rusty is a great husband and father. When we met, he was working as a CFO for a big corporation that I guarantee you have heard of. He went to a prestigious university, graduated with a degree in international business with finance and economics, and worked his way up that corporate ladder. He had done all the right things and was up for another promotion at work. At that time, he had a one-year-old son, and he was already working really long hours.

During a lunch meeting with the CFO of the entire company, Rusty asked about work-life balance and what to expect when he was promoted into this new, higher position. The CFO's response was shocking. The cocky executive spouted off that his overbooked schedule was full a year in advance. There was no time for vacations with his family. The new position would require Rusty to be gone for one month of training, and then he would have to travel three weeks every month. Most people who assumed that role were single or wound up divorced. His direct supervisors even told him the job was "a divorce waiting to happen."

Have you ever had a moment when you realized the dream you were chasing was actually a nightmare? This is exactly what he was experiencing. Unfortunately, this is far too familiar in the corporate world.

How about starting your own business? That can sometimes be even worse. All the time away from your family. The long days where everything depends on you, with no guarantee of success. I believe that most people would love to have their own business. The chance to be able to control your own schedule, do something you are passionate about, and be your own boss is very enticing. Sadly, most people never will, though, because they believe it's too risky. This book is about how to achieve all you dream of within a reasonable price for success. Your business should support and enhance the other areas of your life. Unfortunately, many people's pursuit for a better life can damage relationships and put undue strain on the family and home. Most people have a job, and everything in their life must revolve around it. I believe your family, your happiness, and your wellness are the core and your business is just an extension of who you are and what you stand for.

I want to help you change your legacy. Have you ever thought that you could be the one to change your family's tree? No one in my family was ever successful. Growing up, all my aunts and uncles went through divorces and struggled with money. Neither of my parents or grandparents ever attended college. I had no example of success. Don't get me wrong; I love them, but many of them were unhappy and struggled with addictions and alcoholism. That's not what I wanted for my future. The cycle would end with me. I have a vision that my great-great-great grandkids will have a portrait of my husband and me in their home. They will point to it and say, "Kids, that's your great-great-great-grandma Jaime and your great-great-great-grandpa Shawn. They are the ones who changed everything."

Are you someone who is hungry for change in your life and are ready to go after what you want? Have you felt sometimes it was too overwhelming to juggle all that is on your plate? This book is for driven people who want to win but need to know "how to do it all." I know you are the type of person who has a desire for more out of life or you wouldn't be reading this. The fact that you are holding this book in your hands right now tells me you are smart enough to look for guidance and for the tools to help you get there.

You might be thinking, *Sounds great, but why should I listen to you, Jaime?* There are so many self-improvement and work-life balance books out there. How is this book different?

Let me give you a little background about me. I have been a successful entrepreneur for over two decades. I started with no money in an unfamiliar, male-dominated industry at the young age of twenty-two. I had no experience in my industry or even a college degree. I had moved to a new state and didn't know many people, but by the time I turned thirty, I was making over one million dollars a year. I've built a well-respected business known for its integrity and how we treat others.

Today my company operations have expanded to almost every state and even outside the US. Again, I am in the top fraction of the top 1 percent of income earners in the world. Very rare, especially for a female. More importantly, I have built my business while raising four great kids. I have a fun, exciting, passionate marriage that I am proud of. I have plenty of time for travel, time with family, and community and church activities. I especially love the philanthropic work I do around the world. You get the picture of how busy my life can get. If there is one thing I have a ton of experience in, it's balancing my business and personal life. I can teach you "how to do it all."

I absolutely love what I do, every year growing more passionate about adding value to others. I have been able to change tens of thousands of people's lives, helping them to be better off financially, more fulfilled, and happier. I've coached so many men and women to become six- and even seven-figure income earners. Hopefully, you will be one of the next. So you see, this isn't just one of those books where I *tell* you a bunch of inspiring stories of what other people have done. I've *done* it! I'm *still* doing it! I've helped others to do it, and I can help you as well. Not only *can* I help you but I truly *want* to help you become the next success story.

Let's talk about what you can expect in this book. To truly design the life you desire, you *have* to have clarity. This is where we will start. I will teach you how to create a strong and compelling vision and how to sell yourself on it passionately. My first few chapters alone will give you enough action steps to completely change your life forever *if* you apply them.

In the chapters that follow, I will coach you how to break out of where you are and level up in your personal and business lives. I will teach you my keys to transforming yourself into an effective leader and how to get past some of the traps you will face that may cause you to plateau.

In chapters 9 and 10, you will learn the mindset, the tangibles, and intangibles of building long-term happiness into your busy schedule. I will share with you many of my favorite daily affirmations and tricks to staying focused. I will teach you how to balance everything that you have on your plate and how to have more fun while doing it. We will talk about wellness, increasing your energy levels, diet, and self-care. I will cover how to be more productive with the time you have and share some incredibly valuable lessons in creating wealth.

I will also share with you how to create long-term business stability so everything you are building will be built to last. Finally, we will wrap up with some of the science of happiness to give you tons of ways to become happier now. The chapters in this book are a blueprint to build a successful business and a lifestyle of passion, freedom, and true joyfulness.

At the end of each chapter, you will have many new ideas to try out. I promise there will be a lot of tangible action steps you will want to apply to create real change in your life. I will give you room to brainstorm, journal, and create action items. I hope this book inspires you, gets your creative juices flowing, and expands your thinking. Write in it, jot down any inspiration or ideas that come to mind, and especially take note of anything you want to implement for transformation.

One of my biggest dreams is to touch one hundred million lives, either through the education I do with financial literacy or by building people up as strong leaders who can, in turn, serve and lift others. It could also be through my many philanthropic efforts or through helping them become happier and more successful. This book is just one small piece of that vision. Even though we don't know each other yet, I do care about what happens in your future. You will get to know me a lot better through the pages in this book, and someday, hopefully, we will meet, and you can share your amazing stories with me.

My friend, I hope to add value to your life today and for your posterity to come. My wish is that by applying the principles you learn here, your life will improve in ways you never imagined. I hope to help you to create multigenerational success and prosperity. We are going to have a lot of fun as I let you into my personal life a bit. By the time you finish this book, you will be an empowered, better version of you. You will be on fire with passion and enthusiasm for what you are about to make happen! You will have the vision and a plan to create your dream marriage, family, income, and business. You will also know how to balance all the wonderful endeavors you choose to take on, and you will be on your journey to building a life you absolutely fall in love with. You will be on your way to becoming Happy & Strong! Now that you know what you are in for, are you ready? Let's get started.

1

IF I CAN DO IT, YOU CAN DO IT!

I cannot save the world; that's not what I'm trying to do. I guess I'm just trying to walk the walk and be an example to those that want it. Not everybody does, but if Mary J. Blige can come out of that same hole you are in, then you can do it too.

MARY J. BLIGE

If you are reading this book, I am guessing you have big dreams and want more out of life than your current situation. You are working hard but desire more happiness and fulfillment. I'm excited that you are hungry for change and ready for personal growth.

I'm even more excited that I get to be a part of it. I hope this book will inspire you to use these tools and to take action.

I'm definitely not an expert at balancing; no one is. I'm still a work in progress. I'm not claiming to be the best parent or the best business guru either. But I have built a successful business as an entrepreneur while raising a family. I was making a seven-figure income by the time I was thirty, then continued to grow it as my family grew.

I want to help you find more balance as you pursue your dreams and add more joy along your journey. Before I get into all these fun ideas and action steps, I want us to get to know each other a little better. Maybe someday we will meet, and you will be able to share your story with me. For now, I want to share a little of who I am with you. The main reason for this is I want you to know that if I can do it, you can too! There isn't anything special about me. Everything that I will teach you is doable.

I want to help you find more balance as you pursue your dreams and add more joy along your journey.

So here we go.

My parents grew up in Venice, California. Their families had very little money. Both had alcoholic parents who were physically and verbally abusive. My dad's mom was so abusive that she threw him out of a second-story window when he was a child. She saw him throwing paper out of the window and flew into a rage.

She screamed, "Do you want to throw stuff out the window? How about I throw stuff out too?!" Luckily, my dad's older brother caught him by his pant leg and was able to pull him back up. She abused my dad and his siblings regularly.

My mom's dad dished out harsh punishments as well. He would kick, punch, and one time even put my Uncle Ronnie's hands on the hot stove as a punishment. Ronnie was badly burned and was relocated to a boys' home. It was there that he met my dad, who was also put in this same boys' home. They were both neglected and abused boys and became fast friends.

That's how my mom and dad met. They all hung out and got into trouble together. My parents fell in love, and sometime later my mom became pregnant with me. Shortly after I was born, they decided they didn't want to raise me in Los Angeles and moved to Montana. They, like most of us, dreamed of a better life.

I grew up in northeastern Montana. Have you been there? I doubt it since there is nothing there. Freezing cold Alaskan winds, sub-zero winters, and scattered farms. They do have the most beautiful sky though. That's why it's called The Big Sky State. I miss the Montana sunsets.

It was the tiny town of Medicine Lake. I was a skinny, knock-kneed, homely-looking girl. My baby-fine hair always hung straight and stringy. I called it my "white trash" hair. It's OK for me to say *white trash* since I was white trash. I wore secondhand clothes that never quite fit right. I always felt a little awkward and wasn't sure where I fit in. I guess that's true of most of us, especially during adolescence; we're not really sure of our place. I wasn't talented at anything, and that nagged at my self-esteem a lot. I was a decent student but definitely not one of the "smart kids." I was terrible at sports. I had no musical abilities whatsoever, and I had a hard time trying to figure out "what I wanted to be when I grew up."

I remember one time, in ninth or tenth grade, there was a talent show in the nearby town. Of course, it never crossed my mind to sign up for it. One morning, in algebra class, I turned around to talk to friends at the desk behind me. My friend Kathy said, "Pierson, you should do this." She showed me the flyer for the talent show.

Pierson is my maiden name, and it's what I was usually called in high school. Kathy was always a good friend. She was the homecoming queen and popular and always nice to everyone. I thought for sure she was joking about the talent show. Honestly, it might have been a joke; I've never been 100 percent sure, but she encouraged me to do it. I went to a few of the meetings and discovered it wasn't for me, but this was the first time in my life that I felt like someone believed in me. It was the first time that anyone had ever said I should try something, other than maybe the vegetables on my plate. It felt great to get past my comfort zone.

Later I joined the speech and drama team, entered a couple of poetry contests, and found that my courage to try new things grew. I never stood out though and definitely wasn't a star in anything. One funny thing happened in tenth grade; I was recognized as the Poet Laureate of our sophomore class. I beat out my straight-A, know-it-all friend Shaun, who always won all the academic awards in our class. It was so embarrassing when the English teacher had me kneel down in front of the room. She took out some weird sword and pretended to knight me. "I dub you Poet Laureate of the class of 1995," she said as she dropped the sword down on each of my shoulders. My face was bright red. This was one of the few things I ever got recognition for in school. That's about it. There was nothing particularly special about me growing up.

Medicine Lake is a little town only a few streets wide. Actually, there weren't any streetlights or street signs. My address was P.O. Box 3. If you drove by on the highway and you weren't looking for it, you would most likely miss it. The population was only 325. Yes, you read that right. Not 325,000 people. Only 325 people. It was more like a ghost town. I went to a K through 12 school and my graduating class was eighteen people. Yep! Eighteen people and I'm pretty sure we all graduated. Want to hear something really funny? Our mascot was the Honkers. I'm a Medicine Lake Honker. If you are not from a Podunk northern Montana town and don't know what a honker is, it's a Canada goose.

Medicine Lake isn't the gorgeous scenery and mountains that you see of Montana in the movies. It's nothing but flat wheat fields as far as you can see. We had two bars, a post office, and a little grocery store called Jack and Jill. There was absolutely nothing to do. I'm glad I grew up there, although it's strange because I can't pinpoint why. We didn't have much. My dad worked in the oil field. If that sounds glamorous in any way, it's not. He was always in and out of work, and we survived on government help. We grew our own garden, hunted for meat, had food stamps, and received occasional handouts from my dad's friends.

My parents are Toni and Dan. My mom and I have always been pretty different. I was shy and uncomfortable most of the time, and she is always the life of the party. She always wants to have fun. My dad is very quiet and distant unless one of his favorite old songs comes on the radio or you get him talking about something that fires him up. The summer after second grade, my parents were fighting a lot. There was one really big fight because Dad had gone on a deer-hunting trip. It wasn't until recently that I found out the trip was actually a drug run. He was selling cocaine for extra money.

That day is still so clear in my mind. My mom was sad. After my dad left, she sat me down and looked in my eyes and asked, "What do you think about moving to California?" For a seven-year-old, that sounded awesome—Disneyland, beaches . . . but I was confused.

"Where would we live?" I asked.

"With Grandma! But Dad isn't coming with us," my mom said.

Again, total confusion. I didn't understand why I was feeling so uncomfortable, scared, and sad.

She then said, "It's up to you. You make the decision. It's your choice if we stay here in this place or we go to California."

I thought about it for a minute and said, "Well, OK, sure, let's go. Dad doesn't really pay attention to us anyway when he's home. He just reads his magazines."

I regret that I said that. For months after we got to California, I cried myself to sleep missing my dad. For years, I carried the guilt of thinking it was my choice and my fault my parents got divorced. Over the years, I went back and forth between my mom in the city and my dad in Montana. Every few years I would move. This contributed to a constant feeling that I didn't quite belong. I'm not a city girl, but I'm not all country either. They both eventually remarried. I am my mother's only child, but my dad had five more children after me.

Don't let anyone tell you that you can't have it all.

Years later, I remember moving back to Montana with my dad; his new wife, Gloria; and her daughter, Melissa. My mom was overwhelmed as a single working mom and thought I would be better off not living in the scary area we lived in. She had started dating the man who is now my stepdad, and they both thought I would be better off with my dad. I was grateful for any time he spent with me, but my dad spent most of his time working on cars or tinkering in the garage. He still had no money. We lived in a trailer on the edge of town that had a different color of carpet in each room—red, mustard, and green shag. There was horrible visqueen plastic on the windows to keep the freezing cold winter out. The vinyl kitchen floor was peeling up, and the drawer for the silverware was missing its face.

I hated looking at these things and thinking, *How poor are we? We can't fix that stupid drawer?* I could hear Dad and Gloria at the kitchen table late at night arguing and trying to figure out which bill they could pay. They fought about how much debt they were in. My dad would suggest asking for another loan from the credit union to help them get by.

I knew that wasn't the life I wanted. I wanted joy in my home. I wanted no financial stress. I wanted a nice house that wasn't falling apart. My husband and I both grew up watching our parents argue about money.

After high school, I returned to California for the last time. The idea was to get a job and pay my way through college. I had no car, so I filled out a job application at every business within walking distance. I ended up with two jobs: Blockbuster Video and the 99 Cents Store. I took all the hours I could get until I saved enough to buy a horrible, used '89 Dodge Daytona. It was an ugly brown color with primer on the side and holes from pulling out dents, but at least I had freedom.

Don't let anyone tell you that you can't have it all. There is a secret ingredient that separates the champions from everyone else. (I'll cover this in the next chapter.) It's not which college you went to, it's not which side of the tracks you grew up on. It doesn't matter if you were born rich or dirt poor. It's not about your upbringing, the way you look, the way you talk, or a score you got on a test. Anyone can have the life they desire. Believing this is such an important part of winning in life. I want you to flush out any limiting beliefs you may have from your upbringing. Maybe you grew up in a house where money was "the root of all evil" or where "money doesn't grow on trees." I was told things like "These are the cards we were dealt, and there's nothing we can do about it." A mindset that money is hard to come by or that money is evil does not serve you.

I've helped people from all backgrounds, nationalities, and education levels completely change their lives. Some who are now making six- and seven-figure incomes could barely afford gas and food when I met them. I love hearing success stories, especially of underdogs. I hope you will be one of those stories. Remember, if I can do it, you can as well. I want you to accept that it doesn't matter where you came from, all that matters is where you want to go.

2

HOW BAD DO
YOU WANT IT?

*When your desires are strong enough, you will appear
to possess superhuman powers to achieve.*

NAPOLEON HILL

You have to want to win in your life so *badly*! Winning can't just be something you are "interested" in. It can't just be something you would like or hope would happen. Everyone around you should know how badly you want it. They should be able to see it in your eyes. I wanted everyone around me to feel my conviction in what I was doing. I hoped they would say, "I have never met anyone more determined than Jaime." This mindset comes from belief. If you believe, those around you will start to believe, support, and even follow you. A couple of the affirmations I read daily are "No one wants it more than I do!" and "Everyone around me knows how much I love what I do!"

If nothing changes, nothing changes! Ask yourself, *Am I living the life I have always dreamed of*? If not, how badly do you want change? Have you heard the saying, "You can lead a horse to water, but you can't make him drink"? It means you can give someone an opportunity, but you can't force them to take advantage of it. I've seen plenty of honorable people fail. You may know tons of talented, broke individuals. But what if you could make that horse thirsty? Add salt to his oats, and he will drink. How do you salt your own oats? How do you keep yourself thirsty and motivated? I will teach you how to turn your goals into *musts*.

After being able to make enough to buy a car, I got a better job at a health club. Bye-bye, Blockbuster Video and 99 Cents Store! I thought the gym would be an easy, no-brainer type of job while I put myself through school. I outworked the other employees and was promoted to management in a short period of time. In two months, I passed up people who had been there for years.

Despite my success, the health club wasn't the environment I had pictured. It was a stressful, high-pressure job that I didn't love. I worked ten to eleven hours a day, sometimes six or even seven days a week. After about four and a half years, I hit an income ceiling. I couldn't make more money, but even worse, I felt like I had stopped learning and growing.

Have you ever been there? You get up, go to work, do the same thing every day, go home and go to bed, just to do it all again the next day?

Bored, tired, and unchallenged, I felt like I was wasting my life. I wanted to do something more with my time and energy. I wanted to make an impact and start growing again. In my heart, I knew I wasn't meant for this. If I could put my energy into something I loved, I knew I could be successful. But what?

At this point, I was only twenty-two years old with no college degree. I had no time in my current schedule to go out looking for a new job. But if nothing changes, nothing changes. I knew if I didn't make some serious decisions and take some risks, then I would be miserable.

Are you happy with your current situation? If not, ask yourself, *What will my life look like five years from now if I don't make some serious changes?* I thought of my situation at the gym. I thought of my career in the best possible scenario five years into the future, even ten years. It wasn't what I wanted. I thought of my supervisors who had been there ten years longer than me. No, thank you, I did not want what they had. They were unhappy working a job that gave them no satisfaction. They had no control of their time and worked for a company that didn't appreciate them. Someone else controlled their paycheck and when they could see their kids. Worse yet, most of their incomes weren't much higher than mine. Nope, I wanted out.

Wanting more out of life is normal. I wanted a better quality of life. I wanted to have control of my time, to do what I wanted, when I wanted to do it. I wanted to help others, to have purpose with my work, and most of all I wanted to be in control of my income and my future. No one was going to have their thumb on me anymore. When I was growing up, my dad would go on and on about how he hated his job and how the employees were mistreated. I always wondered why he didn't quit. I learned later that jobs were scarce. He would be in and out of work, and we would go long stretches of time living on welfare. He would complain about the weather, the lack of jobs "in this godforsaken country." Again, I would wonder, *Why don't we just move?*

See, most people want more out of life—but they don't want it badly enough.

I want to *do* more and *be* more! I've always been this way. The one word in the English dictionary that I absolutely hate is the word "settle"! I never want to settle for less than my dream. My dad settled for harsh working conditions on the oil derrick. He worked over 120 feet off the ground on a one-and-a-half-foot-wide metal platform that's called the diving board, guiding the drill deep into the earth, day after day, night after night, working in high winds and sometimes thirty degrees below zero. I can't imagine any worse working conditions. He was risking his life daily at work for little pay, only to be laid off when that hole finished. He has broken almost every bone in his body. He fractured his pelvis, both hands, and his collarbone, and he has had fingers completely ripped off. Why? Life gives you what you *settle* for.

The good news is, life also gives you what you are willing to fight for. So again, how badly do you want it? How badly do you want a world-class, passionate, loving marriage? Or will you be casual, like most people, and settle for an average one? How badly do you want great kids and a strong family? How about a dream career and a life that is exciting, fulfilling, and making a difference? Even when I was little, I was always doing something to make money. I collected cans to recycle, babysat, and even bartended by mixing drinks at my parents' parties. By nine, I made a perfect Jack and Coke. They paid me fifty cents each time I brought them a beer or filled their cup. I'd make crafts and get my little sisters to help. They loved that I was hanging out with them, and I tried to get them to sell the things I made. My poor sister Melissa was the victim of child labor.

When I was in third grade, I was living in California on Venice Beach. We lived in a studio apartment, and my mom couldn't afford for me to take classes like dance, music, or karate like my friends. Because it was practically free, I was allowed to be in Girl Scouts. I'm competitive, so I was the "top camper" and had a sash completely filled with every badge you can think of. When it came time to sell cookies, I was all in! I was the top Girl Scout cookie salesperson. Man, I wanted to be number one so badly. I made my mom take boxes to work each day on the bus. I set up tables outside the grocery store on the weekends, but it wasn't enough. I had some tough competition.

There was a girl named Fatima who was new to our troop. I can still remember exactly what she looked like. She was a tall Indian girl and always looked so serious. I thought she looked like a mom. Fatima rarely smiled or joked around, and she only ate the healthy snacks at the meetings. (Back then, I was a big fan of donuts, and anyone who preferred carrot sticks over donuts was a little suspicious to me.) Fatima had a huge family, and they were all buying cookies to help her out. No one in my family could afford extra cookies. I was lucky if I could guilt trip one of my uncles into one box of Caramel Delights! Even then, I had to make sure to collect the money up front.

Again, I enrolled some child labor. This time, it was my younger cousin, Trisha, paying her with Thin Mints. I would make her walk with me up and down the streets of Venice, knocking on every apartment door. We even went down to the beach boardwalk, dragging a sack full of display boxes. About half the time, she couldn't go, so I would go alone. So dangerous. I can't believe I did this while my mom was at work and even sometimes into the evening. I sold so many cookies to complete strangers and had a couple of scary close calls with weirdos. I'm sure a lot of people bought cookies simply because they felt sorry for me.

The cookies finally came, and it was time to deliver them. Our little apartment was so small and filled wall to wall with cookie boxes. They were stacked floor to ceiling. You had to squeeze through narrow paths in our cookie maze to walk to the bathroom or refrigerator. It looked like one of those episodes of *Hoarders,* but instead of junk and trash, it was cookies…*everywhere!*

The night of the big troop meeting I was so nervous; I couldn't stop biting my nails. My troop leader was a tall, sweet blonde. She always tried to make sure everyone received recognition, so I wasn't sure what was going to happen. She brought donuts that night, but I didn't even take a single nibble; my stomach was so tight with nerves. I listened anxiously all night long as she gave out each pin and badge. Finally, she ended with the top cookie sales.

As I walked up to receive my award, my heart was pounding, and I remember the look on Fatima's face. Most of all, I remember how I felt. The pride in accomplishing something I went after. I knew I worked hard, but I had never received recognition for anything before in my life. The humiliating knighting ceremony in tenth grade didn't come for several years after this. There was no prize for my cookie sales, only another badge on my sash, but I had not settled, given up, or made a single excuse. It taught me that I can hit my biggest goals *if* I want it badly enough!

People ask me all the time, "How do you do it all, Jaime?" It's simple. I don't. You don't have to do it all. I'm completely sold out to three things. Only those three. They are my faith, my family and my business. Early on in my journey to conquer my dreams, I made a decision to cut out things that did not serve me. I cut out hobbies, TV shows that I loved, and hanging out on the weekends partying with friends. When I started out in business, the popular show on TV was *Friends.* I completely stopped watching this show that I thought was so fun. Watching TV was a waste of time, a mindless way that I relaxed. Five years later, after I had hit some of my biggest goals and dreams, I finally got to find out if Ross and Rachel ended up together. A small price to pay for success.

If it doesn't grow my faith, family, or business, I don't do it. There are only twenty-four hours in a day. These are my most important priorities in my life. Now, don't freak out because I didn't mention fitness and wellness. I will cover those later. But these are the top three for me, especially while I was in the foundational phase of building my empire. Sound boring? No hobbies? Well, once you make it, you can do whatever you want, whenever you want. You can take a cooking class in Italy if you think that's fun.

You know what's more fun? Vacationing with my family to Hawaii every year is fun. Not having to worry about money? Super fun. Taking a private jet on a date night is a blast! I don't regret any of that "price-paying time." I made sacrifices and didn't go to the lake with my friends or join the book club that met once a week. You can travel, be the PTA leader, golf, or take up any hobby that sounds exciting once you get the foundation laid. For now, you only have a limited time to get your dream off the ground.

You don't find or reach happiness, you create it.

When I say "faith, family, business," it means the time spent with my kids is quality time, not mowing my lawn or washing my car. When I'm doing things for my church responsibilities, I want to do my best and magnify the role I have been given, whether that's teaching the youth, cleaning the church, or any other service. Let's talk about what I mean by faith and why it is my top priority. To be successful, you must work on yourself. Faith is the best way I have found to do that. Years ago, my good friend and mentor, Ed Mylett, told me, "A sign of a strong leader is they are growing closer to God." It doesn't matter the religion. I have coached and mentored people to win in business from every background, religion, and beliefs—Christian, Buddhist, Jewish, Scientologist, and tons of others. I love people, and I believe we are all more alike than we are different.

No matter your belief, striving to get your spiritual life in order helps. Not only are you happier but you seem to develop a "superpower" for overcoming trials. You become more optimistic. People like to follow others who have vision and the faith that they will get there. People who are growing spiritually seem to bounce back faster from setbacks. Over time, they seem to increase more in self-discipline. For me, my faith is my top priority, and I know it has had a huge impact on why I have achieved this level of success in life.

We can talk more about this later but know you can't "do it all" if you have tons on your plate.

This might be a good time to mention *focus*. Let's say you do truly "want it badly." What should be your focus when you are obsessed with a big goal? If you want to be happy, then happiness should be the focus. Do you have a vision of your ideal life? Not just to make money or live in a big home, but a vision of what you really want when it's all said and done. I hope it's to have the nice things you want, but more important is that you have a vision of happiness and fulfillment.

Many people search for happiness from outside factors. "When I get married, I will be happy" or "When I get a raise, I will be happy" or "After I move, I will be happy." They think some thing or some event in the future will finally bring them happiness. This isn't how it works. You don't find or reach happiness, you *create* it. Doesn't it make sense that this should be the focus? Most people spend way too much time focusing on their problems. They wake up every day thinking about them. They worry and fret about possible scenarios that could happen. They talk about their problems with others. They walk around all day with a voice in their head saying, "This is hard," "I can't," "I'm not good at..."

These become affirmations. Have you ever caught yourself thinking or saying, "This is so hard" or "I'm so tired?" I used to do this. I would catch myself, usually while hunched over in a pathetic-looking posture, saying, "I don't feel good" or "I'm tired." Then I would stop, stand up straight, and consciously say, "No, I feel great," "I'm excited," or "I'm happy." My new favorite affirmation is, "I look great, feel great; I'm in the best shape of my life." Letting problems be our dominating thoughts will destroy our drive and happiness.

Some people focus so much on their problems, they even take them to bed with them—worrying through the night and developing poor sleep habits. Imagine for a second a wife goes to bed and brings someone new to sleep between her and her husband. No good, right? Well imagine she comes to bed with her problems that she's been focusing on all day. She thinks about her problems all day. She talks about them. She's now bringing them to bed with her husband to talk and worry about. This destroys happiness and puts stress on the relationship. Not to mention it stomps out all the passion in the love life. No fun. Leave the problems at the bedroom door.

It may seem like I am always able to stay optimistic. Well, first of all, I'm not always. I have plenty of bad days. I'm still working on these things too. But instead of focusing on where I am, I'm obsessing on where I'm going. Develop a daily habit of thinking, obsessing, and dreaming about your ideal happy life and dwell less on what's going wrong in your current one. What you think about, you bring about! Focusing on your problems will only manifest more of the same. Instead, focus your attention on where you want to be.

The last thing I will say about wanting it badly is you have to be willing to make sacrifices. This dream life you desire won't happen overnight, and it won't happen on its own. Early on, I was willing to work for free to learn my industry. Shawn, my husband, slept in his car for months. He quit his job to be able to put more time into building the business. He barely could afford to eat. He worked side jobs to pay bills and put gas in the car.

After scraping by for months, we were finally able to rent an apartment. It was six hundred square feet. Our bed hardly fit in the bedroom. We rented it because it had a clubhouse we could use for free, and we thought we could hold business meetings there. We had a small kitchen table, a couch, and a TV given to us from a family member. We never hooked that TV up so it didn't work. We were eating ramen noodles and wondering, *Will this ever work? Will we make it? Are we going to make money and get this business going?* During that time, we worked on faith. We went $60,000 in debt, paying our rent some months on credit cards. It drove me nuts. Anyone who knows me understands I despise debt.

When we were getting married, we had no savings. Friends wanted to help me start planning. They gave me their wedding planning books and recommended florists. I saw what they had spent and was in shock. Neither my parents nor Shawn's could help us out financially. We were 100 percent on our own, and I didn't want a penny more of debt. To tell you the truth, as big of a plannerholic as I am, I didn't even want to waste time planning a wedding. I loved Shawn and was ready to marry this man of my dreams. But wedding planning seemed like a distraction at the time. We were both so focused on building the future that we were sold out to.

I set aside all the nice recommendations from friends and said, "Let's qualify for the company Hawaii trip! We can get married there!" It sounded like a great idea to me! We could still stay focused, have our dream wedding on the beach, and our parent company would pay the bill. We put our heads down and busted it for the next six months.

We qualified for the trip to Kona, which is still my favorite place in Hawaii. All I had to do was send the hotel a picture of what I wanted the bouquet to look like and book a hair appointment. I rented a gorgeous dress for only $500 and talked the dress shop into letting me keep it a little longer than usual. We had our dream wedding on the beach for only a few thousand dollars.

Shawn had to get a cosigner so he could finance my wedding ring. Later in the month, family and friends threw us a reception. Of course, they were broke too, so they rented the Disabled American Veterans center. It's the cheapest place in town to rent for an event. It was Hawaiian-themed since it was too expensive for any of them to be at our actual wedding. We all had on Hawaiian shirts. So funny to look back on. Shawn's mom and her friends made turkey sandwiches and sides for the guests. A family friend deejayed for free. On the way to the bathroom, we would stop to chat with a veteran or two having a beer. At the end of the party, Shawn and I helped clean up. We had to save money on cleaning fees, and most of our guests had already left.

Be willing to make sacrifices, get creative, and do without. Most people are not willing to sacrifice temporarily to be able to have what they want long term. In fact, many don't even know what they really want. I will help you with that important step in the next chapter. Are you willing to make sacrifices today to lock in your tomorrow? How badly do you really want it?

To this day, even though I can afford it now, I still wait at least six months before making a big purchase. I do zero impulse buying. Usually I will set a goal to hit, then reward myself. For example, when I bought the home I live in now, I did only a few upgrades. I had new carpet put in and paint, things like that. I set goals to hit before doing major changes. Later, Shawn designed our dream backyard. He put in an in-ground trampoline, skate ramp, and a Hawaiian resort-style swimming pool. It's an eight-acre dream playground for kids. We had talked about this backyard for years, and every detail was in our business plan. We created it first in our mind, back when we lived in that little apartment while eating our ramen.

One of the things I didn't do when we moved in was remodel my kitchen, master bedroom, or bathroom.

Let me tell you how hideous they were. The guy who built this house loved orange. Everything was a terracotta orange color. The walls, tile, counters, light fixtures, the flowers in the driveway—all orange. Even the hardwood floors had an orange tint. I could have easily written a check and taken care of the whole thing. (At this point, I was making a couple million a year in income.) But as much as I didn't like it, I didn't remodel. It's not because I didn't want to or because I couldn't afford to. I wanted to set a big goal to push myself to a new level. I have a habit now of making myself earn things I want, so I have to set a new goal each time. I had to look at the ugly orange stone around my bedroom fireplace for years.

If you want it badly enough, you will have it. Life gives us what we demand of it. It also gives us what we settle for. I don't settle, but I also don't need immediate gratification to be happy. I understand the Law of Sacrifice. To get something of greater value, you must be willing to give up something. There is no such thing as something for nothing. Success, not earned, is short-lived. So don't cut corners; pay the price that real, lasting success demands. You are in this for the long haul, and the vision is happiness.

On the next page is your first action step to complete. Once you identify the time you are wasting, you can allocate that extra time toward making your dreams come true.

ACTION STEP

It's important to know what you are willing to give up to make your dreams come true. What are some things you are doing weekly or daily that are time wasters that do not serve you? Write down those things here and add up all that wasted time.

_____

_____

_____

_____

_____

_____

_____

_____

_____

_____

3

KNOW WHAT YOU WANT!

*I can teach anyone how to get what they want out of
life. The problem is that I can't find anyone who can
tell me what they want.*

MARK TWAIN

Let's chat a bit about how to chase down your dreams. How does a simple girl from Montana get to be a multiple seven-figure earner?

First, you have to know what you want. That can be so hard sometimes. Maybe you were one of those people who always knew what you wanted to be when you grew up. That wasn't me. When I was in high school, the only thing I could even imagine doing as a career was a high school English teacher. I felt a little lost. I knew there was no money saved for college. No one ever talked to me about college prep.

My grades were pretty good. I usually made the honor roll, but going off to college seemed so out of my grasp. I didn't believe it could happen, so I never asked someone for help. Toward the end of my senior year, I really started to feel hopeless, like I didn't belong anywhere. It was embarrassing that most of my friends had decided which colleges they were going to. They were going to be teachers, engineers, and farmers. I was still wondering if my dad and stepmom would even show up to my high school graduation ceremony. They had never come to any other school event I had. Unless you count the time my dad showed up to my classroom when I was in third grade.

I had to dramatically change the direction of my life. There was hope again for a better future.

"Jaime, come take your medicine," he said as the whole class paused and looked toward the gruff voice. I looked over to see him standing in the doorway holding up a bottle of Kaopectate (diarrhea medicine) in one hand and a metal spoon from home in the other hand. *Oh my gosh! Are you kidding?*

For a few seconds, I tried to pretend he wasn't talking to me. The teacher just stared at me until I finally stood up, mortified, and walked out to the hallway. I wanted to literally die rather than make the long walk back to my seat.

I kept imagining that graduation day. All my friends having their little parties with their families. I would have to go to my high school graduation by myself.

When it was time to take senior pictures, I did. When it came time to plan senior prom, I helped. But when they started planning the graduation after-parties to be held at the fire station, I couldn't take it. I decided to leave. I had this overwhelming feeling that if I graduated in Medicine Lake, I would somehow be stuck there. I had to get away. I flew to California and finished the last few months of my senior year at a high school where I didn't know anyone. It was easy because I already had enough credits to graduate. That was a dark time of depression. It was sad not walking across the stage with the friends who I had known since kindergarten. It didn't matter, though. I had to dramatically change the direction of my life. There was hope again for a better future.

I started taking some general ed classes at Los Angeles Pierce College, a local community college in Woodland Hills, California. The information was what I had learned as a freshman in high school, so boring. I was wasting time again. It wasn't for me. I needed to make money now. Again, I felt alone and had no one to give me direction; professors lectured, but no one inspired me.. I still had no idea what I wanted to do.

I only knew what I didn't want. I didn't want to be poor. I didn't want to fight with my future husband over money. I didn't want to have to say no to my kids every time they asked for something. I didn't want drugs, alcohol, and depression to have a place in my home. I also didn't want the decisions I made for my family's health and well-being to depend on how much money we had.

When I started working at the gym, I still had no long-term plans. It seemed like an easy, no-brainer type of job to pay my bills while I was attending those lame college classes. I figured that a gym is a place where people are trying to improve themselves. So it must be a positive environment, right? So not right. It was a high-pressure, salesy meat market. I worked long hours with no recognition.

My first day at the health club, I was so excited—it was such a giant step up from working at the 99 Cents Store and Blockbuster Video. Far from a dream job, though.

The gym was so dirty. We had to kick people out of the jacuzzi in their underwear on a regular basis. So gross. I called the police often because guys on steroids in the weight room would body slam each other WWE style. And don't get me started on the nasty ladies in the steam room with their loofahs, scrubbing their bare-naked crevices. I can still smell the mildew and sweat that permeated the halls nonstop. It was like I lived in an aerobics room where 150 people worked out all day and no one ever opened a window. One crazy night a stray bullet from a gang shooting landed about three feet above my head. I was sitting at my desk when the window shattered and glass flew all over the room. None of that mattered, though, because I had a "real" job, and I was fired up.

On day one, I met the assistant manager—a cute, bubbly blonde whom I will call Cindy. Cindy tried to teach me the basic gym sales lingo and how to answer the phone, and she told me about how fun it was going to be to work there. I was only a few hours into my first day when the sales manager, a woman I will refer to as Karla, gave me a "walk-in"—I guess she figured trial by fire. A walk-in is when someone interested in joining the gym comes in to inquire about pricing. *(I have changed some names here because the behavior at this gym was so bizarre. I know these women wouldn't act like this if it wasn't for the heavy stress they were under.)*

I looked at her and said, "But I don't even know how much memberships cost." She handed me a flyer and said, "Take them on a tour of the club, then show them this." Awesome. I smiled and went upstairs with my potential sale.

I gave them a tour even though I personally had never used any gym equipment in my life. I was kind of a skinny-fat person. I looked thin but never worked out ever and was soft all over. I couldn't last five minutes on one of those treadmills.

"Here is a great machine for the triceps," I said as I glanced at the sign on the tricep press. After the tour, I took the well-dressed businessman and his wife into a sales office. We talked about their fitness goals for a few minutes, then they asked about a commercial they saw on TV. It was an ad for nineteen dollars down and nineteen dollars a month.

"Yes, our best pricing of the year," I said. We talked for a few more minutes, and they said they liked everything and would be back tomorrow to sign up. Awesome! Great first appointment under my belt, or so I thought.

About ten minutes later, I saw Karla in the hallway. She was shorter than me but fit. She had legs like a running back—many years of step board aerobics classes was my guess. Every salesgirl there looked like they taught spin classes on the side.

"Where did they go?" Karla snapped.

"Oh, they loved it, and I set an appointment for them to come back tomorrow," I said, smiling.

Instantly, Karla grabbed my uniform and pushed me up against the wall. We all had to wear these ugly uniforms. Silky warm-up suits that zipped up the front. They looked like giant hefty bags with a teal stripe going down the legs and across the chest. They made a loud swishing sound as we walked and were impossible to look cute in.

"A 'be-back' never comes back!" she screamed, about four inches from my face.

I thought I was fired for sure. She was definitely not the same nice girl I had met in the job interview two days before. This giant rage monster was pinning me so tightly I couldn't move. My feet felt like she had lifted me off the floor. I looked around to see if others witnessed the savage attacking me near the front desk.

"They never come back! Never let them leave! Not without talking to me first!" she yelled even louder.

Well, I wasn't fired. I quickly learned this type of insane behavior was a normal occurrence with the stressed-out managers. I worked my butt off and got good at sales so I wouldn't be taking that kind of abuse ever again. Two months later, I was the assistant manager. About a month after that, I was promoted to manager and transferred to another location, where I soon became number one. I moved to a cleaner club in Encino, California. No stray bullets flying into my office from gang shootings in the parking lot. No more WWE and no nasty loofahs in the steam rooms. But Encino was a whole new animal. I finally experienced the culture shock everyone warned me about when moving from Montana to California.

I was not expecting the people. Some of the most stuck-up people I have ever met in my life worked out at that gym. I almost preferred the gang members over these snobs.

Encino had a huge book of written complaints, and daily it was getting bigger. As the manager, I would be called up to the front desk for every upset whiner. I couldn't believe what I was hearing and in the snottiest voices.

"The paper towels don't come out right when I pull on them. Fix it by the next time I come, or you will hear from my attorney."

"I had to wait five minutes for a treadmill." Oh, poor baby. "I don't like what's playing on the TV." Every day.

"The free weights don't re-rack easy enough." I wasn't even sure what that meant, but each time I would tell them I would take care of it.

Today we would call these ladies "Karens." One time, a gorgeous blonde with a perfect body, very fashionably dressed, came up to the front. As soon as she opened her mouth, she wasn't pretty anymore. In the most spoiled, bratty, snippy voice, she said, "Make this car move, please!" She handed me a paper with a license plate written on it. She wanted me to read the license plate number over the loudspeaker.

"Sure, is it blocking you?" I asked.

"No, it's just ugly and old and I'm afraid they will dent my Mercedes!"

It took some time getting used to this type of environment. In Montana, people were friendly. Of course, we had our share of gossip, and everyone in town knew your business. It's hard to keep secrets in a small town, but at least everywhere you went, people smiled and waved. We left our cars running when we went into the grocery store, and we left our front doors unlocked at night. You can imagine the culture shock dealing with this Miss Priss and people like her every single day.

At the gym, I usually worked eleven hours a day. We rarely took breaks to leave the club. I ate my lunch quickly in a back office between appointments. I was making more money, but after four-and-a-half years there I still didn't know what I wanted. But I knew what I *didn't* want. I didn't want to waste my life at a place that never appreciated my efforts. It didn't matter if I was number one. They repaid me by raising the "budget" (their word for quotas). I'm still grateful for my time there. I learned how to deal with crazy people, and I learned how to manage people way older than me. I worked like a self-employed person, even though I was an employee.

> *I knew what I didn't want. I didn't want to waste my life at a place that never appreciated my efforts.*

The women at the Encino gym would come in, full makeup on, looking amazing in expensive workout clothes. After their workout, they would go upstairs to the luxurious Skin Spa, one of Southern California's hottest spas at the time. It seemed to me that they didn't have a care in the world, aside from how slow the paper towels were coming out, of course. They had rich husbands, and they didn't have to work. They would drop off their horrible, nasty kids in our kids' club. That's a role I never had to fill, thank goodness. I used to call them the Bebe's kids. They would bite and throw things and never listen to any of those poor girls who had to sit in there and watch them.

One day, a woman who was a regular at the gym came and found me in my office.

She was in her fifties and looked like a million bucks. It was obvious that she was wealthy. It might sound weird, but she even smelled amazing even though she had just finished working out. Her hair, her nails, her shoes, everything looked impeccable. I adored her cute blonde bob haircut. I found out later her husband was a man who owned the high-end, luxury car dealership nearby.

What now? I thought, waiting for the next off-the-wall complaint. This time, for once, it wasn't a complaint.

"Oh good, you're here," she said in an exotic accent.

Of course I was there, I *was always* there. I practically lived at that gym. She pulled out a pair of black leggings from a plastic bag. "I thought these might fit you. You are always working hard, and I see you. These don't fit me, and I thought you might like them."

She put them in my hand. They were such great quality, so soft and thick. Way nicer than the ones I was wearing that I got on sale at Target.

"Yes, I would love these; I bet they're the perfect size." I happily took the treasure, and she smiled and left.

At that time in my life, for some reason, I was so touched that this stranger would give me a gift. I had never met someone like her. She was rich, beautiful, classy, kind, and so thoughtful. Later, as I tried on the leggings, I noticed how nice they smelled. Is this what rich people's houses smell like? I wondered. Hilarious but true. She probably traveled the world, went out to fancy dinners, and stayed at five-star hotels. She didn't worry about her hooptie-car breaking down. I wondered about her luxurious lifestyle.

Finally, *I knew what I wanted!* A goal, a vision, started to become clear in my mind. I called it "The Spa Life"—I wanted to have what these rich housewives had. I wanted not to have to worry about bills. I wanted to travel the world and have complete control of my time. I wanted never to have the pressure of financial stress!

I wanted to have the beautiful clothes and nice cars and dream homes. I wanted to go to the spa all day if I wanted to. I wanted to be rich. I wanted all that these ladies had, but I also wanted to be like the gracious woman who so kindly put those leggings in my hand. I would use my money to lift others, *and* I wouldn't get it by marrying some rich guy. I would build my own spa life through hard work, perseverance, and dreaming big.

From that moment forward, I began to grow dissatisfied. I wanted more. I was sick of doing the same thing over and over again. Never making an impact! I hated going home to that little apartment and not being able to save money or help my parents. I had no desire to hang out on the weekend anymore, drinking and going to the same places. More than anything, I was sick of struggling and watching my family struggle. My antennae were up for new opportunities.

A friend of mine who was in real estate suggested I get my license, so I did, and realized very soon that it wasn't for me. I didn't like the thought of driving people around and being at someone's beck and call. There were too many things outside my control that could affect my pay. I tried being a loan officer and processing mortgages for a while, then stumbled into my current business when I met a nice lady at the gym. It was perfect timing. My boss, whom we called "Satan," had just asked me to transfer back to that original crappy gym I first started in so I could "fix it." The gym where a bullet came into my office three feet above my head…the one with WWE and loofahs. I wasn't happy about it.

This is how they repay me? I thought. I've worked like a slave every day. I am number one in the company, and they send me back to that crap hole to fix it?

But I did what my boss asked and went back to work at that location. I was there only a few days when God intervened. A woman came in for a tour, and it changed my life forever.

Arlene was a sweet, soft-spoken Korean woman. She had just given birth to her second child and had never worked out before. After trying to sign her up on a membership for about twenty minutes, she left. They never come back, remember? Well, she actually did. (Thank goodness.)

After talking to her husband, she came in to sign up. As I was typing in her name and address, she complimented me.

"You are so nice and good with people. Have you ever thought of doing something else?"

Only every day, I thought.

"Yes, I'm actually looking into other things and doing mortgages on the side," I said, trying not to sound desperate. "Why do you ask?"

"Well, my husband has a business, and he is looking for some good people."

I was so excited. I felt like I had been "discovered." I was so ready for change, but I tried to act cool and not too excited. I asked her what kind of business it was. She was so cute.

She leaned a little closer to me and said, "It's securities. It's very lucrative!"

What did she just say? My mind searched for meaning. I had never heard the term "securities." Was she talking about home alarms? Security guard? No, that's dumb.

I quickly responded, "Wow, sure I'd love to meet him." I was so hungry for opportunity. I'm sure you have been there, desperate for a change of scenery.

That was the moment I was introduced to my current industry. I fell in love with financial planning. I loved that I could control my own schedule, help families in so many ways, and make good income. I also loved the personal development culture of the office where I worked. Soon I was exposed to so many incredible business leaders. First was Arlene's husband, John Shin. He challenged the thinking that was ingrained in me from my upbringing. He challenged me to get outside my comfort zone daily. Most of all, John and others helped me to get clarity on what I wanted my life to look like. I wrote my first business plan. I wanted to stretch myself and "think *big*!" I wrote down that I wanted to make $10,000 in a month. No one I knew made that kind of money. Was it even possible?

Fired up and looking for help with my plan, I brought it to John.

So John is a lot different than his wife, Arlene. Not soft-spoken. He is super intense, direct, charismatic, and has a flare for the dramatic. I sat at his desk as he read my plan, thinking he would say, "This is awesome, Jaime, you can do it!" or something encouraging along those lines.

About halfway through, he looked up at me. He stared at me with an expression on his face like, "Are you kidding me?" It reminded me of Dwayne Johnson, The Rock, when he does that raised eyebrow thing.

"This is crap!" he said, raising his voice.

Huh? What was happening? Was he mad? These guys were always so nice to me. I was silent and shocked. He tossed the plan on the floor and looked straight in my eyes.

"What do you really want? Look around you. Look at what is possible. You need to get clear on your 'whys' and what you really, really want," he said.

Back to the drawing board. I guess I wasn't thinking big enough. I left his office with that written plan laying there on the floor. For the next few days, I spent time digging a lot deeper. Was it just my "spa life" vision I wanted? What were my "whys?" I was still only twenty-two, had no kids, and frankly it annoyed me that "being successful" wasn't a big enough *why*.

I started by forcing myself to write at least ten nonmonetary reasons why winning was my only option. My ten *whys*! You may have heard something like this before, but have you actually done it? Have you searched your heart to find what lights your soul on fire?

I wrote pages about the places I wanted to visit, the dream home I wanted, and financial independence. Not much emotion, but at least I was getting clearer on what my "spa life" looked like. I invested time into myself by digging and digging to figure out who I was and what I wanted. Gaining this clarity made me more and more excited. A few days into this process, I was on number eight! I found my *why*!

It didn't matter where we came from; all that matters is where you want to go.

My number-eight *why* was "I want to win in business and life to be an example to my younger siblings." I wanted to show them that it didn't matter where we came from; all that matters is where you want to go. I loved them more than anyone at that time and felt a little like I had abandoned them in Montana. I'm the oldest of six. I have a stepsister, Melissa, two sisters in the middle, Jessica and Danica, and two unexpected twins who came along years later, a boy and girl named Tessa and David.

My stepmom, Gloria, has had serious health challenges since the twins were born. She's undergone about fifty surgeries and was heavily addicted to the narcotics the doctors prescribed.

There is a big age gap between me and my siblings, and I always felt a sense of responsibility to help with them. All ten reasons on that list got me excited, but this one made me emotional. Now as I set goals, it wasn't just a business plan; I had an emotional game plan.

One thing champions will do is dig deep to figure out what emotionally charges them. You can do this too. I promise it will change your life if you invest the time. Create your list of *whys* that *must* happen and use it as fuel to push yourself to new levels. I wrote goals into my plan about exactly how much I wanted to make and by when. I detailed the things I wanted to do for my family and the dream life I wanted to create. I had short- and long-term goals, serious heart-wrenching goals, and all my fun, exciting, wildest dreams. I included exact dates of when I wanted to have every one of these things. I read my plan every day, first thing in the morning and last thing before bed. Each time it refocused me and filled me with the passion and conviction I needed.

You are probably thinking about people and goals that stir your emotions. If you are working hard and making sacrifices, write down the names of those individuals whom you are doing it for. Maybe a parent or someone who you want to help. Maybe a child you want to provide a better life for. Also, write down your most important goals that make you emotional. This will help you identify your whys and reasons for winning.

I put photos and pictures that I ripped out of magazines up in my apartment that would remind me of my vision and my whys. I wrote little phrases on my bathroom mirror and in my note-books. I even stuck some of my goals on the steering wheel of my car. You can do this too. Keep your desires in front of you as often as possible to remind yourself of why you are paying the price. It reminded me of why I was working all day and night and taking all the rejections. Most of all it helped me fight the negative, nagging voice in my head. That voice made me doubt I could ever amount to anything special.

Each time I had to do something uncomfortable, such as a client presentation to someone older, I would look at a picture of my sister Danica. Sometimes, I would sit in my car, dreading going into a client's home because I felt I wasn't good enough. I had to remind myself that my little eight-year-old sister Jesi was making dinner for twin babies. I would imagine her in a dirty house while her mother was lying in bed in the other room, drugged up on meds.

If you don't do it for them, who will? Your whys push you out of your own way.

One of the keys to setting goals that has made the biggest difference for me is the idea of thinking bigger! Once you have a written plan and goals, try to challenge your own thinking. This was hard most of the time for me. Remember, I grew up around small-town thinking. Nothing big ever happened in Medicine Lake.

The county newspaper would post the police reports boasting big stories like, "Last night someone drove down Main Street with their headlights off." Seriously, no joke. One time the headline read, "Someone broke into a parked car in front of Jack and Jill last night. No damage, but a frozen chicken and bed frame have gone missing!" That one still cracks me up.

When this is the most exciting news, people get used to the "same ole, same ole." They settle, and small thinking is the norm. So each time I have a plan or goal I ask myself, "Is this big enough? Would it inspire those I intend to help and serve?" Think of others who are where you want to be in life. Ask yourself if this is a goal they would have had when they were in the stage you are now.

Last, compare your goal to what is possible. Usually, as big as our goals may seem, someone else has achieved them. We have our excuses of "If I didn't have kids, I would set a higher goal," or "If I lived somewhere else," or "If my health were better," or "If I had more support." Sorry to tell you, but whatever excuse you come up with, someone with that same excuse is crushing it right now. Stop looking at your current circumstances, skills, and what you have done in the past. Instead, look at what is possible. Remember, records are meant to be broken! So *think bigger*. Rewrite your plan. Set new goals. Become an impossibility achiever. Do this "think bigger" process over and over again if you have to. Do it until what you are reading to yourself is so exciting and inspiring and even a little scary to think about.

You might have heard this quote from Machiavelli: "Make no small plans for they have no power to stir the soul." If you are going to become an impossibility achiever, your soul must be stirred. You can't wait for a book or motivational speaker to fire you up. Tony Robbins and Ed Mylett are such great inspirational speakers. As good as they are, even on their best days, they can only give you the tools to help you make change. They can get you excited, but they can't do it for you. That motivation will eventually wear off. The only true motivation comes from within. *You* must learn to motivate *you* long term. You have to light your own internal fire and keep it raging. Where there is no passion, mediocrity sets in, and that is where you will stay.

Stop looking at your current circumstances, skills, and what you have done in the past. Instead, look at what is possible.

OK, my friend, once you have a vision of the dream life you desire and clearly defined goals, you need a written plan. Once you have stretched your vision to the point of almost impossibility, your hair is practically on fire. You will know it's the right plan because you are so lit up about what is about to happen in your life you can barely sleep. You stop wasting time, and every extra moment you are consumed with your vision.

Keeping it in front of you all the time is the next step. Read it, visualize it, absolutely obsess on all the amazing things you are going to do for your family. Keep stoking that fire. It's too easy to become distracted or apathetic again. Once you hit a goal, create a new vision. If the plan you are reading doesn't have the same effect anymore, create a new one quickly. When you crush your target, you will be a different person who is capable of new and bigger things. Don't slow down. Don't become complacent. Keep rewriting your future. Keep chasing a better version of you.

OK, so you have already written down some of your whys. Now write down some of your *big*, selfish, seemingly impossible goals. If money were not a factor, what would you be doing with your time?

I see so many unbelievably talented people work hard and achieve so much, and then one day they just stop. They plateau. Some at $250,000 income (that's a common goal for some reason); some once they buy their dream home or achieve a big "why." It kills me to see this. This often happens because their inspiration was only about themselves and their personal goals. If you create your vision about helping or serving others, then you never stop. You draw more and more energy from the people you serve. You will never "arrive" and never plateau. You will keep growing, learning, and, most importantly, you will continue to feel fulfilled.

OK, let's get back to reading your goals. It's important that you emotionalize your goals in the morning and at night, at least twice a day. Try using something as a trigger. Figure out something you do every day, like walking out the door or brushing your teeth. Every time you do it, it starts a movie in your head of the life you want.

If you have a goal of retiring your mom, then you should be able to clearly visualize the day you tell her she can call her boss and quit. You might envision the weather outside, cold or hot. How does she react when you tell her how much money will be deposited every month in her bank account? All the thoughts and desires you can imagine vividly, mixed with emotion, will start to manifest into reality.

Try your hardest to see and feel yourself already accomplishing the goal. If it's a dream trip to Hawaii that you want, visualize walking on beach, feel the sand on your toes and the sun on your face. What does it smell like? How does your spouse look in that tan? Put all the juicy details into your fantasy. This helps stoke the fire to increase your desire. I also keep a copy of my goals in my shower. (Hopefully you take showers every day.) It's perfect. All you have to do is laminate your plan, get it wet, and it sticks to the wall. That way if you forget to read your goals in the morning, they are right there as you wash your hair. It saves time by killing two birds with one stone. My kids think it's funny when they hear me reading my affirmations out loud in the shower. I've even gone through stages where I would flip the water to freezing cold and yell out my goal. I can get pretty intense sometimes, but it's because I want it badly.

I know it's not always easy to envision your dream life when things are rough. When we were still struggling in business and in debt, it got so bad for a while that Shawn and I stayed at my mom's house.

Late one night, after a horrible day at work, I told Shawn I was going to quit. All my appointments that day flaked, some of my little team had quit on me, and a big client canceled his plan. The worst part was an unethical agent (who is now in jail) had hurt our business to the point I wasn't sure we could repair it. I was overwhelmed and completely over it. Shawn, the annoying, eternal optimist looked at me and almost laughed.

"You won't quit!" he said with a smile.

"Watch me! You can do all this crap yourself!" I snapped. "Let's see how that goes!" I was getting mean now.

He stayed calm but didn't know what to say next.

"I'm done!" I said as I turned out the light and went to bed without looking at my goals that night. It was the first time in months that I had gone to bed without reading my plan first. I laid there for a while tired, hurt, and sick to my stomach. I sobbed in silence as my thoughts fought to occupy the space in my head.

Really? What made you think you could do this? Who do you think you even are? You are letting everyone down.

I started to beat myself up even more.

All this time and money wasted. All the people who told me I couldn't do it were right. I'm living in my mom's house. What a loser! I tried to sleep but couldn't. Shawn, of course, was out as soon as his head hit the pillow. It drives me crazy that he can fall asleep so fast.

After about a half hour of torturing myself, all my goals and business plan started to fill my mind. It was like someone had pushed play on a recording. The same plan I had been reading morning and night for months. The affirmations of the person I was becoming came next. Instead of that negative little voice, it was a strong, powerful, encouraging voice.

If you don't do it for them, who will?

I thought of Dani and Jesi asleep in their beds 1,500 miles away. I thought of my dad.

If you don't help him retire, who will?

I even thought of a young girl named Jennifer. She was recently hired, and I had sold her a big dream of how she could win and help her own family in Texas. I couldn't quit on any of them. I crept out of bed and rummaged through the stack of papers on the floor. I found my goals and snuck off to the bathroom. I stood there on the cold bathroom floor as I read my plan out loud. Tears streamed down my cheeks.

"I am the hardest-working person I know! I deserve victory! I will be a hero to my family, clients, and teammates!"

I read the whole plan again and again until I could feel it in my entire body. I would never quit! I got louder until I was practically yelling it out loud. I didn't care who I woke up, my heart was so full. I went to bed that night at peace and full of hope, fueled again by my own dreams. The next morning, I was the first one in the office. A few months later, we were debt-free, and I had crossed over $100,000 in income.

ACTION STEP

The most important part of goal-setting is that they are written and read daily. So before you continue, create your first draft of your vision and plan. The important part is not that it is perfect; the important part is that you start. Some people spend too much time creating a long, elaborate plan that they don't take action on. Others don't invest enough time, and their plan is too short and doesn't stir their soul. Start brainstorming your rough draft here.

_____

_____

_____

_____

_____

_____

_____

4

IF YOU'RE NOT GROWING, YOU'RE DYING

Failure is success in progress.

ALBERT EINSTEIN

Do you ever feel stuck? Hit a ceiling in income or there are no longer any growth opportunities in your career? Is your relationship losing its fire? Maybe you're bored with your current life, nothing to challenge you, and it seems like an endless rat race. There is an old saying, "I'm sick and tired of being sick and tired." I've been there. Every time I sold a gym membership, it was like cement hardening around my feet. Getting unstuck is no easy task, but it is an important skill to learn to build a dynamic, rewarding life. Even if you are a little slow at times, you must keep moving forward.

There are several ways to create more happiness in your life, and one of the biggest is progression. The definition of progression is "the processes of developing or moving toward a more advanced state." That is essentially what you are after here, a more advanced state of being. More balance, more productivity, more time, more wealth, more lifestyle, right? The lack of progress in your life will cause you to feel stuck, uninspired, and unhappy. For this reason, it's so important to keep new and exciting goals in front of you.

People used to say things to me like, "You work too much!" or "When will it be enough?" These same people would lie on their couch, binge-watching movies and TV shows, complaining about their jobs and everything else in their lives. Their discontent prompted them to take jabs at my lifestyle. No, thank you. I'm busy, but I love that I am chasing the next version of me, and I'm constantly progressing. Stay inspired by continuously stretching your vision and updating your objective. It will fill you with the passion and enthusiasm that develops from making an impact instead of the lethargy that comes with an apathetic mindset.

Stay inspired by continuously stretching your vision and updating your objective.

When you lack clearly defined goals that move you, it's easy to just drift through life. I want to remind you that this book is only for those few people who actually have the drive and determination to make their dreams come true. Very few people ever really follow through on their dreams.

Do you feel that way sometimes? Just drifting. "This year looks a lot like last year." This is why most people never really accomplish anything great in life. As kids, we are all *big* dreamers. If you ask my five-year-old what he wants to be when he grows up, he might say a firefighter, a baseball player, and Iron Man. There are no limits to their imagination.

As we get older, we learn to shrink our dreams and settle. We drift through life letting years go by until we are just sick and tired and ready for change. But by then, opportunities have already passed us by. Most people apathetically drift. Don't let this be you. I love the quote from Dr. Martin Luther King Jr.: "Whatever you do, you have to keep moving forward!" Fight for consistent progress. Break your goals into bite-sized, daily action steps and attack them.

I have four categories I do this in. I call them the four *F*s: Faith, Family, Fitness, and Finance. I'm not sure who I heard this from the first time. It might have been my good friend Monte Holm. I have had several successful multimillionaires tell me they have similar categories. These can be short-term, long-term, big, or small goals. You define the goal, then create the actionable steps.

Faith can be any spiritual or self-improvement goals. Some of mine over the years have been things like reading scriptures daily, service projects, and smiling at others more. Again, you're striving for progress, not perfection.

Family goals can include any relationship-oriented goals you have. I've written down goals like not yelling at the kids, showing enthusiasm when Shawn walks in the door, and even potty training a little one. There is no wrong or right or too small or too big.

Fitness is obvious; it's improving your health. I usually have eating better, exercise, and self-care in my plan. I will get into more details on these in later chapters.

The last category is *Finance*. This is where you will include goals and action items involving your spending habits, savings, business objectives, and net worth.

It's important to do all four categories for many reasons. For one, it helps keep you balanced. I am super competitive and driven. When I'm going for a big career milestone, I'm all in and laser focused. When I read my four *F* goals and track my progress, it constantly rebalances my attention so I don't become too much of an off-balanced maniac.

For long-term happiness, you must be personally growing in each of these four areas. Again, who cares if you are making millions but you ruin your marriage, your kids don't talk to you, or you have driven your health into the ground? Keep tracking progress, celebrate little wins, reward yourself, cross things off to-do lists, and give yourself credit for every gain you make. This will build not only confidence but contentment.

Progress is also important for our self-worth. As I pointed out earlier, it is so easy to be lazy and to be apathetic. Usually, it's not because you are a lazy person but because you are bored from lack of desire and progress. We, as humans, gravitate toward the path of least resistance. We take the easy road, mindlessly flip on the TV and veg out, pour a glass of wine, and complain about the day. Self-discipline is hard. We might have a goal to lose weight or save money, but we have our same old habits. When I worked at the gym, every January it would be packed. People would set their New Year's resolutions to get in shape. It was my sales team's busiest month of the year. We would sign up more new memberships in the first weeks of January than any other two whole months combined.

The lines for the treadmills would be so long. People would have to work in with each other and share a machine in between sets.

Of course, at Encino, I'd get complaints nonstop.

"You are overselling this place! Have you seen how crowded it is?" But every year, without fail, by the third week of January, it was back to normal. This is why I never make New Year's resolutions; they don't work. We lack self-discipline! When we set goals and then don't follow through or progress, it wears down our self-image. Our self-image is how we see ourselves. It determines if we truly, deep-down believe in ourselves, and if we don't believe we can *have* something or *be* something, it's not going to happen.

This is why self-discipline, habits, and progress are so important. Setting a goal is like making a promise to yourself. If you keep breaking these promises and letting yourself down, you lose self-respect. Your self-worth and self-esteem start to deteriorate, your self-confidence is diminished, and discontent grows. This is how I felt at the gym because I had stopped learning and growing. Day in and day out, always the same thing. Lack of progression.

So what's the solution? How do you become more disciplined like the champions you admire? They are not superheroes, and they have the same twenty-four hours in a day as you. How do you stay consistent so you don't end up like those New-Year's-resolution gym members? (You know, the ones who signed a three-year contract and paid thirty dollars per month for thirty-six months and went only five times.)

It's pretty simple actually. I'm going to share some tips that most people won't do. You will follow through because you are ready, hungry, and want it badly, right? It's how someone like me, a poor girl from Montana, became one of the top-earning females in the world. It's a big secret to success and to happiness in general. Remember the action steps I mentioned earlier? The goals in each of the four *F* categories? OK, here it goes. *You know what you should be doing!*

You know if you want to be healthy, you should eat right, exercise, and get enough rest. If you neglect any of these three for too long, you will get sick. When hitting a savings goal, you have to spend less and save more. In your business, you also know exactly what you should be doing to win. Knowing and doing are two different things. If success and self-discipline were easy, everyone would be successful. They'd be happy living their dream, and there would be no need for you to read this book. Having self-discipline is saying no to the dessert, making the extra calls, or not letting yourself buy something so you can save the money instead. It's becoming a master of your habits instead of letting them master you. Willpower and discipline are not something you are born with; they are something you develop.

So here's how it works:

1. Identify what needs to be done or what you should be doing to win.
2. Recognize what you are actually doing.
3. Focus on narrowing the gap between the two.

Let's say the top producers in your business make about one hundred calls a day, and you make an average of eight. You can't expect to have the results they have. Start to narrow the gap. Make it a point to increase your self-discipline and your capacity. Progress daily, narrowing the gap of what you are currently doing and what you know you should be doing to achieve your goal.

> *Willpower and discipline are not something you are born with; they are something you develop.*

Start to keep the little promises to yourself, and you will begin to cultivate a stronger self-image. You start to see and believe that you can do what they are doing. Same with any other goal. It's self-improvement. This works if your goal is to drink less or quit smoking. It works in relationship goals to be kinder to family members. Narrow the gap of what you know is right and what your current behavior is. It works for fitness as well. For example, after months of working at the gym and selling memberships to people, I figured I should start working out. I'd been selling people the dream of how this equipment will change their body and their life, but I wasn't doing it myself. I made excuses, like most people do: "I'm too busy! I'm too tired. I don't have any time with this crazy work schedule."

Finally, I got serious.

First, I asked one of the trainers to help me through a workout. Bad idea. Our personal trainers were not certified. They were basically guys I had hired to re-rack weights and wipe down the sweaty machines. A huge creatine junkie named Claude coached me through his "ultimate leg day." The next day my calves cramped up so bad that I couldn't stand up. I was lying on the office floor begging one of the girls to rub them. I couldn't sit down without pain for three days. It's funny now, but it wasn't funny then. I didn't quit though. Eventually I got on a routine. I worked out every day, six days a week. I started doing kickboxing, lifting weights, and running stairs. I built my dream body, just like I built my dream business and life. With self-discipline! As my legs turned into Jell-O from running flights of stairs, or when I felt like throwing up during an intense martial arts workout, I would remind myself to "eliminate the competition."

Most people quit when they get tired or it starts to hurt. But I didn't want average results like everyone else. I kept going, increasing my determination and belief that I could accomplish my goal. It wasn't too long before I achieved the body I wanted. I've done this in every other area of my life as well. If you can have discipline in one area, you can have it in any area. When I want to win at something, I eliminate the competition.

I'll give you an example. I started at my company, broke and at the bottom. There were tens of thousands of people already in the company, and they all had more experience than I did. Most people would look at that and get overwhelmed. That's a lot of competition. Wrong! I already had extremely high self-esteem and belief because I had learned how to close the gap! I knew I had developed the will to win, so it was only a matter of time. Most of those people couldn't compete with me. Not because they weren't talented but because they lacked discipline. I figured out who the real players were (typically there are only a few). I figured out what exactly it took to win. Next, I defined the reality of where I was and what I was doing. Then, I narrowed the gap.

This all may sound so tough; after all, discipline is not really a fun word. But if you followed my earlier instructions and figured out what your emotional motivators are, it's easier than you think.

Narrow the gap of what you know you should be doing and what you are actually doing.

Self-discipline is fueled by inspiration and passion. Narrow the gap of what you know you should be doing and what you are actually doing. You need to outgrow yesterday and grow into tomorrow. Each day make progress and increase your self-image. This, my friend, is real self-improvement. It's not just listening to podcasts and reading books. It's you making personal progress toward the man or woman you were meant to be. There are two of you. There is the guy/gal that is and the one you are meant to become.

There is an amazing woman I have coached in business for years named Dana. When we met, she and her husband were newlyweds and both had just been laid off. The company they both worked for decided to move out of the country to save money on cheaper labor. She was desperately looking for change in her life, and I believed in her. She was positive, energetic, and easy to mentor. She duplicated everything she saw me do almost instantly. Dana progressed so fast that I started calling her my rabbit. Have you ever seen the greyhound dog races on TV? When the dogs race, a fake rabbit shoots out in front of them, and they all take off running after it. That was

Dana. She took off so fast that everyone else I was coaching started to pick up their pace as well.

It wasn't long, and her next step in progression was to speak publicly on stage. I coached her on a simple topic, and she was assigned to train for ten minutes on a Saturday morning. That morning she couldn't sit still. Dana paced nervously in the hall. When she was introduced, she inched to the stage and looked around the room at the fifty faces staring at her. She stood at the podium fidgeting and chewing gum. One of the first rules of public speaking is don't chew gum on stage. I giggled to myself as she held tightly to the podium and the overhead projector in front of her as if someone was going to pull her off the stage.

Do you remember the old overhead projectors? The ones with clear transparency paper and markers? I hated those things. They were big and clunky, and they always burned out at the worst time. I made so many last minute office supply runs for those stupid bulbs. As Dana taught the group, I sat in the back row observing and ready to cheer for her at the end, no matter what she said. She leaned forward and started to draw out a diagram on the overhead, nervous and excited at the same time. Just as she started to gain confidence, her gum fell out of her mouth onto the transparency in front of her. Of course, it was turned on and projecting a giant, gross blob on the wall behind her for everyone to see. She froze. All eyes were on her, waiting in suspense to see what she would do next. After staring at it for a few seconds, she grabbed the wad of gum and put it back in her mouth. I was dying in the back of the room; it took everything I had to not fall off my chair laughing. The girl next to me almost peed herself because she was laughing so hard. One of my other guys then walked up to the front of the room with a waste basket and held it out in front of her. She smiled, threw away the gum, and kept on training. When she was done, we all gave her a standing ovation. Dana's a champ. That embarrassing incident could have stopped her from trying again. She had a few more uncomfortable moments over the years, but she kept getting better. She kept progressing and is now one of my favorite female speakers. Dana has absolutely crushed it speaking in front of more than thirty thousand people at a time. She is a caring leader, an incredible mother, and a hugely successful businesswoman. She didn't let this one embarrassing moment get in the way of achieving her dreams.

The happiness you gain when you keep progressing, eventually closing the gap to become the second you, is worth it. I won't ever promise you that winning and developing a Happy & Strong lifestyle is easy. I can tell you it is so worth it.

As you are growing, you will face choices and associations that will help or hinder that growth. It's the little things that can make all the difference in the world. Avoiding stepping on land mines while on your way to your destination is a monstrous part of why high achievers dominate in their fields. This next chapter is key to that, and I can't wait to share it with you.

ACTION STEP

Write down any major areas in your life where you would like to have growth in order to achieve your dreams. What do you need to do more or less of to become the person you want to be?

_____

_____

_____

_____

_____

_____

_____

_____

_____

_____

5

LEVEL UP

I am who I am today because of the choices I made yesterday.

ELEANOR ROOSEVELT

Our choices today determine our tomorrow. Do you have bad choices that you regret? Yep, me too. Everyone does. It's OK to make mistakes as long as you don't keep making the same mistakes again and again. When you keep repeating mistakes, it becomes a choice.

I had a best friend in eighth grade whom I adored. We were pretty much inseparable. We lived a few doors down from each other and were even born just a few days apart. Even though we had other friends that we hung out with, she and I were always together. We walked to and from school together, did homework after school together, and on the weekends spent the nights at each other's houses. There was rarely an argument between us. We were both pretty good kids, as far as teenagers go. Sometimes I was the one who got us into trouble, like sneaking out to hang out with older boys. Sometimes it was her idea, like grabbing some beers from her grandpa's refrigerator.

I can't remember whose idea it was to go buy our first pack of cigarettes and go to the park that day, but we grabbed her older sister's lighter and headed out. On the way, she pulled out a cigarette and lit it. She looked like a pro, like she had done it a million times. She didn't even stop walking while she lit the cigarette. It hung from her lips, and it seemed she got taller at that moment. I was pretty impressed.

I grabbed the pack from her hand, tapped it against my fingers to make some come out, the way I had seen my dad do for years. I stopped walking and really focused on lighting the end as I put it to my lips and tried to take a puff. I started coughing uncontrollably. It was the grossest taste ever. My head started spinning, and I thought for sure I was going to throw up. No cool points for me.

She didn't laugh; she just sat there smoking her cigarette as if she had done this for years. When I finally stopped doing this half-cough/half-gagging noise, she said, "OK, just suck a little on the end. When you have it in your mouth, breathe in while saying a word."

I thought I might die if I did it again. She then took a big drag, breathing in deep so her chest would puff up as she said, "Mommy," in a high pitched, scratchy tone. *Weird*, I thought, as I robotically modeled her and put the cigarette to my lips. I squeaked out, "Mommy," followed by about five straight minutes of hacking. In my mind's eye, I saw Pinocchio turning green with watering eyes after Lampwick had him try the cigar on Pleasure Island. Where was my Jiminy Cricket? Well, I smoked for about a year after that and then off and on for years. Stupid.

Now, I dearly love my friend, but I'm introducing you to her to make a point. We were so alike back then—born two days apart, lived on the same street, our parents were a lot alike, similar grades, even similar taste in food and in boys. Our lives today are much different. At key decision times in our lives, she made one choice and I made another. She made choices with alcohol, with guys, with her career. I did too. Some decisions were small, others bigger, but each of these choices created a wider chasm in how our lives would end up. Year after year, she made choices, and I made choices until our lives looked nothing alike. I became increasingly wealthier, happier, and healthier while my friend seemed to be going in the opposite direction on many things.

Shortly after I had my daughter Daisy, she called me. She was obviously unhappy. Her career was not going as planned, she was broke, and she had a little girl not much older than mine. She told me the guy she was with had been abusive, and she needed a place to go. It was the worst possible timing. I was going for a huge business goal and working like crazy that month. But I loved my friend, so of course I let her stay at my house.

She arrived with a car that barely ran and a few pairs of clothes. She didn't even have enough money to buy her daughter food and milk. The baby cried so much, poor thing. It was hard to comfort her. My friend would have to take my car and drive her little girl around and around the block to help her fall asleep and pacify the incessant bawling. Shawn and I paid for the needed car repairs and relocated them to live in another state with her mom.

How did we become so different? Even though she is a great person, kind and loving, there she was with no money, no job, no marriage, and no hope. I was about to cross over a seven-figure income, had savings, no worries, low stress, dream cars, and was living happily with my family in an amazing neighborhood.

Each poor decision weighs heavily on your happiness. Choose wisely, for the consequence of each bad choice results in fewer choices next time. For example, a one-night fling now could lead to an unwanted pregnancy, which may reduce the options for your future. Some dumb choice goofing around that leads to an arrest results in a criminal record and fewer job choices in the future. The saddest thing I see is someone hungry to change their life, but they have limited opportunity because of a past bad choice.

The same year I started smoking, my stepdad went to jail. He had been partying and drank way too much one night. My mom had gone down the street to party at another house. He made a choice, the wrong one, and decided to go look for her with a gun. He fired the gun downward, and it ricocheted off the ground and into the leg of one of the guys at the party. He served a few years in prison, years he can never get back.

Choose wisely, for the consequence of each bad choice results in fewer choices next time.

I love my stepdad, Russell. He has always treated me like his own daughter and has taken good care of my mom. Russell has always wanted to do better and improve his life, but he has less opportunities available now because of that night. He is a good guy who had to live with a bad choice. My mom became a single mom again. We moved back to LA, back to a single studio apartment. I would clean neighbors' apartments to make extra money. She was unhappy all the time.

When I say be smart in your choices, I'm not telling you to be too cautious. I want you to go for it. Take risks; go after your dreams! The future belongs to the *bold*. I went full-time in business right away before I even had the proper licenses to make money. I didn't wait until I knew what I was doing or until I had a clientele;

I just went for it. Everyone told me I was making a mistake quitting my job to do something I had no experience in. Just use common sense and follow what your gut and heart are telling you. Too many people are so afraid of making the wrong choice that they blow their shot at a better life.

There was a girl named Mayra who was in my business a few years ago. I loved her kindness, her amazing smile, and her passion to help others. She was good at the business but came from a poor family that was overly cautious. They suffered from multigenerational small thinking. Mayra's husband constantly told her to get a part-time job so they could feel a little more secure. Her parents made her feel guilty that she was pursuing something new that didn't provide a steady paycheck. She finally gave in to his pleading and gave up on all her ambitions. She had big dreams to help her parents retire, send her children to college, and buy a nice home with a backyard.

Recently I was talking to one of my business partners and was sad to learn Mayra is now a housekeeper and is hurting financially. Her whole family is struggling to get by. Lack of choosing is also a choice, and the consequence is regret.

One of your biggest choices as you grow and build your Happy & Strong life is who you choose to associate with. If you haven't heard this before, *you are your associations*. If your friends cuss a lot, you usually will too. If they drink a lot and like to go to the lake all weekend, you usually will too. If they are super negative and complain about their jobs, politics, and their relatives, you may not realize it, but you are most likely a little negative as well.

Try a little experiment. Think of the five people you associate with most often. This could be who you talk to on the phone daily, who you live with, maybe a parent or best friend. Now add up the income of those five people and divide by five. The answer will be really close to your current income. If you want your life to change and you desperately want to become that *second* you, your associations most likely need to change. There is a saying, "If you are the smartest person in the room, you're in the wrong room."

Human nature is to hang out with people who make us feel good or at least comfortable. There is nothing wrong with that; you should feel safe and have fun with friends. If your friends make you feel bad, then why are they your friends? Sometimes, however, we like to hang out with them because they don't challenge us to change. Your true friends love you just the way you are, but a mentor or powerful association will love you enough to help you grow.

Think about those five people. Which one is dragging you down? Maybe they are not supporting your vision for the future, being negative, or causing you to do things that don't serve you at this stage in your life.

Surround yourself with positive, like-minded people.

So how do you change your associations to be happier and more successful? Surround yourself with positive, like-minded people. These people should be supportive about the changes you are making to be better and have a better quality of life. During my first year in business, I started to get scared, and money was low. I confided in Shawn that I was considering a side job doing mortgages. We weren't dating yet.

He looked me in the eyes and said, "You are so close and so good; don't do it."

I needed someone in that moment to just believe in me. If I would have said that same exact thing to any of my friends or family members, it would have been a totally different response. Well-meaning as they are, they would have eagerly agreed with me that it was time to get a job. That small choice could have drastically changed the course of my future. If you have friends who are negative toward what you are doing, let them know that you love them, but you won't allow them to put you down. If you find that some friends are just not on the same path as you anymore, it's OK to not be around them as much or even at all. You change; friends change... that's life.

If it is a spouse who is the negative one, that's different. Sit down and really tell them why you want this so badly. Explain your vision for your family, why this makes you so happy, and tell them how important it is to you. Don't get upset or crazy emotional; just paint a vivid picture in their mind of the dream you are chasing. The most important part: *Tell them you want them to be a part of it and how important it is to you that they are happy for you.*

Bottom line: Find a core group of like-minded people and a mentor or two—people who care about you, and you enjoy being around, who still challenge you in some way. You'll know you are making the right associations because you are happier and want to become a better person as a result. You can have multiple mentors, role models, and, of course, powerful associations through books and audio. You may have one mentor in spiritual matters and another in financial or fitness. You wouldn't ask your financial advisor to be your fitness coach, right?

Here are my rules for choosing a mentor:

• They care about me and have a vested interest in my success.

• They are on the same path I am, just further down.

• If I follow what they are teaching, will I be happy?

• Do I want the life they have?

• They must have good character and integrity. (I wouldn't choose a shady business mentor who beats his wife just because he is financially successful.)

This might surprise you, but most successful people like to help others through mentoring. Sometimes all you have to do is ask.

One important piece of advice: Don't waste their time. If you are fortunate to have someone in the position you want to be and they are willing to teach you, their mentorship is priceless. Their guidance may help you avoid mistakes, which will save time, money, and heartache. So don't blow it; be coachable to them. One of my biggest strengths is that I have always been super coachable. I have made a tremendous effort to find incredible mentors.

I work hard on developing a quality relationship with them and try to add value to them any way I can. When a coach gives me instruction, whether it be in fitness or business or any other area, I implement immediately. You could say I'm coachable "at the speed of instruction." This makes the mentors know their time is not wasted on me, and they should continue to impart their wisdom. I have been able to excel quickly in anything I put my efforts toward because I have the help of others who are already successful.

Here is how you use a coach or mentor:
- Be very specific on the question or direction you need.
- Ask them what they think you need to improve on or focus on.
- Take notes and get clarity on everything they say.
- Take immediate action.

After you get results from implementing the strategy you were given, go back to your mentor and say, "This is what I did. Here is what happened. What's next, Coach?" Those three words accelerated my career more than you can imagine: *"What's next, Coach?"*

If you're a mom and there is some supermom at church, offer to take her to lunch and pick her brain. If there is someone in your industry who you really admire and would love to build a relationship with, maybe secretly call their assistant and ask about all their favorite things (favorite restaurant, etc.). Send them a gift and let them know how much you appreciate their example and look forward to meeting them someday. Include your contact info. Don't be afraid to reach out. These little choices have made me millions over the years.

LEVEL UP

Remember, it's OK to make mistakes. I make mistakes pretty much every day. If you are not making mistakes, it means you are not going for it, not doing enough, and probably not growing as fast as you would like. Failure is part of success. I've failed at all the things that people admire about me now and ask my advice on. Just try not to make the same mistake twice.

If you are not making mistakes, it means you are not going for it, not doing enough, and probably not growing as fast as you would like.

Level up. The next level means ready or not, *charge!* Go get uncomfortable, fail, and come out the other side stronger for it.

Speaking of stronger, the next chapter is about the one thing that can really develop you into a new, better version of yourself. It's the crash course on self-development and growth that no one likes but everyone needs. This next subject we will dive into has helped me become the person I am today. It's the great separator of the old you and the new you. I hope you learn to appreciate it as much as I do. Are you ready? I hope so. Before you move on, take a moment to complete the following action step.

ACTION STEP

Make a list of people in your line of work who would be amazing as a mentor. Who would make a big difference if they helped you in some way? Even if you are nervous, reach out to one or more of them and start a relationship. Do the same for the other Fs (Faith, Family, Finance, and Fitness). Who would be great to get coaching or tips from in these areas?

_____

_____

_____

_____

_____

_____

_____

_____

_____

6

ALL THIS IS FOR THY GOOD

Character cannot be developed in ease and quiet. Only through experience of trial and suffering can the soul be strengthened, ambition inspired, and success achieved.

HELEN KELLER

I woke up and immediately knew something terrible had happened. The air felt sick and stale. The tone in my mom's voice down the hall was new, like a scared animal. I lay in my bed with my eyes open, not wanting to find out who might have passed away or got hurt.

Why didn't they go to work today? I wondered. Was it that bad? I was groggy and tired from getting home late the night before. I couldn't afford an assistant yet, so I had stayed at the office until midnight catching up on admin work. (This was still early in my business when I was struggling with being able to pay bills and we were staying at my mom's house.) I really didn't feel like joining in a negative conversation, so I lay in bed another ten minutes. I could feel the tension and sadness creep down the hall to that back room and find me.

Whatever it was, it was bad, and it wasn't going away. Finally, I threw on some sweats and walked into the living room. The TV was on, and everyone was glued to it in shock. I watched over and over as they replayed the planes crashing into the Twin Towers and the buildings collapse. It was utterly unbelievable. There were no words. Shawn and I looked at each other, not really knowing what to do next. *Is this really happening?* I wondered.

Bad things are going to happen, but you must have the tenacity to keep going.

As distraught as we felt that morning, we took our showers and headed to the office.

We were the only people in the entire twelve-story office building who showed up to work on 9/11. I made phone calls to teammates and clients like I did every other day. Shawn helped three families put a financial plan in place. This was only a few months after getting my securities licenses and opening my own office. I was paying the price that success demands.

My friend, adversity happens. Bad things are going to happen, but you must have the tenacity to keep going. Not long after that day, the stock market began to tank. I was already paying my office rent on my credit card. I wasn't prepared for my business to sink further into debt. Many of the people in my industry became bitter and negative. The guys who started many years before me became easy to pass up on promotions. Hard times became all they focused on, while I just kept working on me and getting better. Become *better*, not bitter.

Soon after that tragic day, I read a magazine article about some of the victims who died in the building where the second plane had crashed. There was a financial firm on one of the floors that the plane entered. Some of the men working there were able to call their family to say one last goodbye. Some had to make a choice that morning to jump or to be burned alive. The article spoke about how the widows were left with no life insurance and had to pick up the pieces of their life and move on.

I looked at the faces of these widows on the magazine cover and thought, *If these people were in the financial industry and that's what they did for a living, why didn't they have their finances and insurance in place?* Being in the financial industry myself, I just couldn't help but think how much more the average family needed help and financial education. This adversity hurt my industry, but it strengthened my passion for what I was doing.

According to Napoleon Hill, "Every adversity, every failure, every heartache carries within it the seed of an equal or greater benefit." I know this to be true. Every adversity carries within it a benefit. As hard and sad and career-destroying as 9/11 was, it made me better in so many ways. I gained more conviction about what I do, became more empathetic to my clients' needs, and was more resourceful looking for solutions. It also prepared me for the bigger personal adversities that would come.

I've had so many hard things happen in life and in business. All champions have. Do you think that the people making millions and the star athletes had it easy? Of course not. Mary Tyler Moore once said, "You can't be brave if you've only had wonderful things happen to you." Courage comes from facing challenges.

There was a bad person in our company who stole from us, making so many of my clients cancel and teammates quit and hurting the brand of the firm I was with. I had to restart several times because of this horrible person. I don't want to say his name, so let's just call him Creepy Carl. One time when I was very new, I overheard yelling and then a loud crash in the front lobby of our office. As I came running out of the copy room to investigate, I saw a huge man pulling his fist out of the wall he had just punched a hole in. I stood there with my jaw wide open.

"Where's Carl?!" he screamed. Carl had a habit of stopping payment on checks that he had written. This guy owned the entertainment company Carl used for a company Christmas party. The check Carl wrote him was one of many that bounced.

Creepy Carl was a dishonest person who eventually went to jail. He lied and cheated, and there was constant drama around him. I don't really want to go through all of that negative war story, but it was one of the hardest challenges I had to overcome. He gave me every reason to give up. From that crazy psycho adversity, I learned what NOT to do. I told myself, I will always do what's right! I would never lie ever, even a little white lie. If people can't trust you in one thing, they won't trust you with most things. I will be fair and honest in all my dealings. No one in my business or in my clientele will ever wonder or doubt my intentions. The experience with Carl was way harder than 9/11, and I became better for it.

Growing up, I had nonstop adversity. I had to be independent at a young age.

My mom lost me one night when she was drunk at a party on some boat docks. I was terrified by myself in the dark for over an hour.

When I was ten, I was molested by an uncle while both my parents were in the next room.

As a teenager, I was left behind in another state because my stepmom "forgot me." I had to find a ride home because she was too tired to drive back and pick me up. This was before cell phones, so I had to wait until she was all the way back home before I even got a hold of her.

Shawn and I have had to help sick family members, we've had children go through learning disabilities, a daughter with Sensory Processing Disorder, massive setbacks, and times of chaos. Adversity will come. Make a decision to win anyway. Make the choice to be happy anyway. I know it's hard to feel grateful for the hard things happening in your life. Know that these hard things are not happening *to* you; they are happening *for* you. One of my favorite affirmations is "All these things are for thy good."

When the tough things come, and they surely will, try to understand that trials, adversity, and hard times are for your good.

Without them, you will never be able to grow into that second version of you that you are really meant to be. The Roman philosopher Seneca once said, "No man is more unhappy than he who never faces adversity. For he is not permitted to prove himself."

> *Hard things are not happening* to *you; they are happening* for *you.*

I know sometimes this is hard to believe, especially when it's the really tough stuff, like the loss of a baby, a friend sick with cancer, or war. You wonder why these things happen. I knew a family with five children and the mom died shortly after giving birth to the last child. So heartbreaking. You can't really make sense of it and surely can't be grateful for the trial, at least not in the moment. In hindsight though, all trials will give us some benefit and experience that is for our good.

When I think of that second version of me, I see someone who can help lift and do so much good for others. To go from where I came from to where I am now, I have had to learn and change and grow. To get to where I really want to go, I have to learn, change, and grow some more. Growth usually comes from hard lessons. I can read books all day long, but some of the best personal growth I have ever had is learning from adversity and my mistakes. Your road to happiness and success is not easy, and it's for sure not a straight line. It's an uphill climb. There will be failures, heartaches, and setbacks. Plenty of victories and celebrations and deep valleys of depression and self-reflection. Be prepared to climb from peak to peak, each time becoming a better version of yourself.

I look back at my childhood and the hard times I experienced as I built my business and wanted to quit a thousand times. I wouldn't change it. Not any of it! It all made me who I am today. It helped me become a compassionate leader who can now help others through their darkest times. I'm grateful for the good times and all the people who helped me, but I'm also grateful for the people who told me I wouldn't make it. I'm even grateful for the market crashes, the sicknesses that my family has had to endure, and people like Creepy Carl and my Uncle Ronnie who made it so hard on me that I had to fight even harder to find out who I really was and what I was capable of becoming. If you are in your valley, look for the seed. Look for the benefit. *Win anyway!*

Lou Holtz, the famous football coach, said, "Show me someone who has done something worthwhile, and I'll show you someone who has overcome adversity." Your trials are a gift. What are you supposed to be learning from this gift?

Have you seen *Black Panther*? It's one of my favorite Marvel movies, although I have a big crush on Captain America and Thor (don't worry, Shawn knows). Do you remember what happened when King T'Challa would get hit or shot? He would absorb the impact, become stronger, and then use that to deliver an even heavier blow! That's got to be YOU. Learn from it; don't complain, "Woe is me." You can bet the adversity will come around again until you DO learn. It will look different, but it will come back around.

I still have hard things happen, and I still have personal growth to go through.

In the next chapter, I will share with you one of the biggest weaknesses I had to overcome and change about myself to be able to reach higher levels in my business and personal life. All the great champions had hard times; they all had death and sickness in their families they had to face, they all hated the grind at first, but they did it anyway. That's why they are winning!

Do you ever wonder why, during tough times, some people just seem to rise to the occasion? I'm so inspired by Winston Churchill's famous quote, "Kites fly highest against the wind, not with it." If there is no wind, a kite can't get off the ground. Opposition helps it to soar.

When the winds of adversity in this life are beating you down, lean into the wind.

When the winds of adversity in this life are beating you down, lean into the wind. Keep pressing forward. Like the kite, this is exactly what you need to be able to rise. You can't fly your highest without the adversity in your life. Lean into the wind, my friend; you have greatness in you! Let this trial you are facing be the refiner's fire that will mold you into the person you have always wanted to be. Become better, not bitter. Decide to win anyway! No matter what adversity comes, you just soak up the impact and get stronger. You are ready for whatever comes next. Choose to be Happy & Strong.

ACTION STEP

What are some difficult things you have overcome in your life, and how did they make you stronger? Write them down here, then embrace these afflictions and be grateful for the strength and/or wisdom they gave you. Remember, if you made it through these tough times, you will make it through the hard stuff happening in your life right now.

_____

_____

_____

_____

_____

_____

_____

_____

_____

7

IT'S GOOD ENOUGH
NOT BEING PERFECT!

*Good enough is good enough. Perfect will make you a
big fat mess every time.*

REBECCA WELLS

OK, so confession time. I'm a total control freak. I should put
the quote above on a T-shirt and make it one of my new
mantras. I have gotten better over the years, but I am definitely a
recovering perfectionist. It made me pessimistic at times. I used to
have to have everything done before I could quit for the day. This
may be useful in getting day-to-day tasks completed, but it keeps
you in small thinking constantly. The thought process is, *If I want
to get it done right, I have to do it myself* or *I will just do it, so it gets
done faster.*

If you are going to build the life of your dreams with total control of your time, you can't be working in the details all the time. You have to be thinking much bigger and staying excited about where you are going instead of micromanaging where you are currently. One of my daily affirmations is "It's good enough not being perfect."

I think the change happened when my good friend Greg Kapp called me one day out of the blue. It's great when you have friends who love you enough to help you grow. Greg is a good man who genuinely loves people. He is much older than I am, and I call him Papa Kapp. My kids actually think he is their grandpa. One time on a Hawaii trip, my son, Austin, kept getting new pool toys his "papa" was buying for him. I was super annoyed that my kid kept asking him for money.

There is no such thing as a perfect leader or perfect parent.... You are striving for progress, not perfection.

Anyway, as I was driving home from the office one afternoon, my phone rang. I looked down and smiled to see it was Greg calling. He probably noticed my compulsive need to be right and perfect all the time, and in the most loving way, he wanted to help.

He said, "Jaime, you are a great mom."

"Thanks, Greg."

I always enjoy his praise; he is one of those people who has the natural gift of encouraging others and making people feel good.

"You're not a perfect mother, and that's OK," he continued. "You are a great leader but not a perfect leader. That's OK too."

I really needed to hear this on that day. There is no such thing as a perfect leader or perfect parent. I needed to stop driving myself crazy trying to reach an impossible goal. You are striving for progress, not perfection.

One of the deadly diseases that causes failure is detail-itis. Most of us have at least a mild case of it. Checking emails, doing paperwork, taking forever to make a decision. Don't major in the minors! Delegate anything that causes you to think smaller and takes your eyes off your vision of happiness. I have an incredible assistant, and one of his jobs is to give me multiple choices when making a decision. It could be something as easy as picking a design for a brochure.

He gives me three or four choices instead of asking me what I think we should do. That way, I can quickly pick one and move on. Leaders are quick to make decisions and slow to change their minds.

Wanting to please everyone is another symptom of this need to be perfect all the time. Are you a people pleaser? Years ago, I threw a company Christmas party. I wanted to have a great party so my team would feel special and appreciated for all their hard work all year long. I got caught up in all the little details of the menu, the decorations, and the entertainment. My staff is perfectly capable, probably even better than I am at party planning, but I wouldn't let it go. I had to have every detail passed by me first.

I had a referral for a great comedian, we had our usual amazing DJ, I was even looking into making it snow over the dance floor. On the night of the party, I was so stressed out. I was literally adjusting the holly berries on the centerpieces.

"Don't open the doors yet! Make sure all the candles are lit!" I said, panicking.

Finally, the doors opened, and people came in. For about half an hour, everyone just talked and hugged and socialized. They were all having fun, but I couldn't sit still. I moved from table to table, making sure everyone was OK. During the dinner, the comedian came on stage. I was mortified; he was terrible! The worst! I wanted to kick him off the stage.

To top it off, there was a mix-up with the entertainment. Several little people arrived dressed as Santa's elves and started handing out candy canes. I felt like I was on that old Ashton Kutcher show, *Punk'd*. I was so embarrassed. Thoughts of firing someone, punching the restaurant manager, and running to the bathroom to cry all crossed my mind. I kept smiling, taking pictures, and watching as everyone else didn't even seem to notice the train wreck I was witnessing. My associates kept on laughing, dancing, and having an amazing night.

When it was finally over and I got into the car, Shawn looked at me and said, "That was fun, huh?"

"Fun? It was the worst! *Ever!*" As I said that, a feeling of worthlessness began to set in. The problem with perfectionism is it's an impossible goal to hit.

Do you remember the *Frozen* movie? Now, whenever I find myself fretting over minor decisions or trying to get things just right, in my head I sing Elsa's song, "Let it goooo! Let it goooo!" Trying to be perfect or please others will steal your joy.

As a parent, I found myself guilty again. I'd be at church on Sunday trying desperately to keep my kids quiet. Another impossible task. I'd be stressed and exhausted bribing them with snacks or pulling the seventh activity book out of my bottomless purse. I would be so envious of the family sitting perfectly still in the front row with like six kids who had perfectly braided hair. Daisy's hair was always a mess; because of her sensory issues, she hated having her hair brushed.

I picked my battles. If she ate and had clothes and both shoes on, we were ready for church. One day we were sitting in one of the aisles far in the back, as usual, and she got away from me. Who am I kidding? This happened more than once. She was so fast. Like a giant, screaming cricket, she was all the way up to the podium before I could do anything.

The speaker was delivering an emotional message to the congregation and didn't notice the little blonde toddler at his feet. Not sure how he missed it; no one else did. I quietly made my way up. I could feel my face getting hot; I must have been bright red. Off to the side of the room, I bent down and motioned for Daisy to come to me. All of a sudden, she began to giggle uncontrollably. It was so loud and high-pitched that it jolted the speaker. She took off, darting in the other direction, laughing at the top of her lungs, and running back down the opposite aisle. I did my best speed walking after her.

I finally caught her in the hallway, grabbed her arm hard, and sat her on the couch.

"What are you doing?!" I snapped at her in my meanest, church-whisper voice. "That is *not* OK!"

She tried to get away, and I sat her back down. "Nope, you have to sit with me now! And no more books!"

She started to cry. Obviously, not a supermom moment. Was I trying to correct my child or was I just frustrated because of my own embarrassment? What is more important, nurturing and correcting my child's behavior or what someone else thinks about me? This is another by-product of perfectionism: caring way too much about what others think of you.

Nowadays, I don't care what I look like as a mom to others. My only care is about the relationship I have with each of my kids and what my Father in heaven feels about my parenting style. So no more bribing with snacks, to say the least. I build my dream life and run my business and home the way I see best without that perfectionist stress or the fear of judgment.

So many are addicted to the approval of others. This is another joy stealer! If you worry about what others will think or say, you give them influence over your future. You can't build your dream life when you hesitate to go with your gut. You will never get your business off the ground because you listen to too many opinions. Just believe in what you do and go for it.

I'm sure you know people who have gone to school to become what their parents wanted them to be instead of pursuing their own dream. Then they end up miserable. Even worse, think of a girl who "decided" to marry the man her dad would approve of instead of following her heart. Sad. Addiction to the approval of others is just another version of trying to be perfect for someone else.

Everyone will have an opinion, but none of *them* are going to fund *your* dream. They are not going to pay your bills, send your kids to college, or buy you that dream home you have always wanted. Nope, all of that is up to you alone. That's why it doesn't matter what anyone else thinks. As I was struggling to get my company off the ground, I was so embarrassed or worried about what others thought of me. Many of them are still exactly where they were twenty years ago or worse. I'm so glad that I gave up on the fear of failure and approval of others and just went after what I truly wanted.

If you worry about what others will think or say, you give them influence over your future.

Overthinking is another symptom of perfectionism. Are you worrying too much? Losing sleep at night? Slow to make decisions? All this does is paralyze you. It keeps you right where you are. It shuts your mouth when you want to speak. Perfectionism is like a thief stealing away the spontaneity and pleasure from your days. Do you ever find yourself lying in bed and you just can't turn off your brain? Trust me, I have a lot of experience with this one. Instead of losing sleep or worrying about things that probably won't happen anyway, read a book for a while. Change gears and give your mind a break. What I have learned to do in these annoying overthinker moments is to give myself some recognition.

"Wow, I've really been working hard lately. That project is going so well. I've spent so much time this week on ..."

You get what I'm saying. It takes you out of distress and relaxes your mind. Try this simple technique next time you can't make your brain shut down. It may take a few minutes of trying to come up with praise for yourself, but you will eventually start to feel yourself relax. Perfectionism is a trap.

You are enough! You have everything already inside you to win big time and be happy.

Jane Fonda said, "The challenge is not to be perfect—it is to be whole." Perfectionism is the opposite of self-care; in fact, I consider it self-abuse. My friend, you are enough! You have everything already inside you to win big time and be happy. It is OK to not be perfect! So just "Let it goooo! Let it goooo!" and get your joy back.

Are you ready for what's next? Brace yourself—we'll go over grit, hard work, and toughness. No pansies allowed. It's what every ultra-achieving entrepreneur has to have to get to the top and stay there. Are you excited? I know I am. But first, complete the action step on the following page.

ACTION STEP

Write down some of the important things you got done this last week, last month, last year.

_____

_____

_____

_____

_____

_____

_____

_____

_____

_____

_____

8

WORK HARD, DESERVE VICTORY!

I'm a great believer in luck, and I find the harder I work, the more I have of it.

THOMAS JEFFERSON

Alright, prepare yourself—this will probably be your least favorite chapter.

You must have work ethic if you want to win. *There is no substitute for hard work.* I know, I know, you wanted to read this book to learn about how to have balance and maybe even work less. You have heard of the "four-hour work week" and want to start living the dream now. That's not how it works. You have to embrace the grind, my friend. The dream comes once you deserve it. So, at least in the beginning, while getting your idea and business off the ground and systems in place, it's good old-fashioned hard work. There is a time period that you just have to bust it and grind for a while.

How hard are you willing to work to have the life you want? Shawn's philosophy was always, "I will work hard now so I can take the rest of my life off." Do you remember what I said earlier about how success demands you pay a price? I prefer paying that price up front and in full. Everyone wants this amazing dream life, travel, and financial freedom, and anyone *can* have it. Most people are just not willing to do what it takes to make it happen.

We are almost to the chapter on how to do it all and balance it all, so hang in there—but I wouldn't be doing you any favors if I didn't tell you winning takes hard work. Stay with me; I will try to keep this chapter short.

How hard are you willing to work to have the life you want?

You can fake it, post on Instagram about how much you are doing, tell your mentor you have been busting it all day working harder than ever, but only *you* know how much you are really doing. When you look in the mirror, you can't lie to yourself. When you know you don't deserve to win, it just won't happen. You know if you are giving something all you've got. When your heart is in the work and then you throw yourself into making the dream a reality, magic starts to happen. When you know that you are doing all you can do, victory will surely come.

Have you ever worked so hard that you felt you could will success into your life? Ninety-plus percent of winning is will, not skill. Vince Lombardi said, "The difference between a successful person and others is not a lack of strength, not a lack of knowledge, but rather a lack of will."

Early in my career when I was still in debt, I was working long hours at least six days a week, driving all over town to do appointments. I was tired and so frustrated. Bills were piling up, and I knew in my heart that I couldn't work any harder than I was. There were many nights I would literally fall on my bed and go to sleep without even washing my face or changing my clothes.

This was one of those days. My back hurt from sitting at my desk from 8 a.m. to midnight that day. My shoulders were tight tennis balls that were stuck up at my ears. I had gone into my closet to change and fell to my knees. I was flooded with emotion. Anger at first. Mad that no matter how hard I worked, my business didn't seem to move. A saying that some of my business partners used to repeat came to mind: "The rapid, relentless repetition of these simple things will lead to an inevitable explosion."

Make a decision that the work is worth it. Not easy, worth it!

I was working so hard. *Where the heck was* my *explosion?*

I'm the hardest worker I know, I thought. *I am* relentless. *Why is it not working?"*

Frustration and exhaustion gave way to tears.

"I want this so badly, and I know I'm doing the right things. I deserve victory."

That night, I knew in my heart that I was giving it my all. Art Williams used to say, "All you can do is all you can do. But all you can do is enough." It's true. When I knew I deserved to win, things seemed to get easier.

Soon after, my business started to take off. Within weeks, I was over $100,000 in income. The right people and circumstances appeared. Training and mentors came to my aide. When you know you deserve success, it comes. You are building your story. An incredible story of a life you designed. There must be a challenge, a struggle, a good fight, and *then* victory. Make a decision that the work is worth it. Not easy, *worth it!*

Hopefully, you can find work you love, like I did. Then it's not really work anymore. One thing all the top two-percent income-earners have in common is they have unbelievable passion for what they do. It's more than making money. Today, I can do thirteen appointments and not be tired. I'm actually energized by it because I feel I'm helping and serving others. I'm fueled by the people I pour into.

Plus, if your work is only about you or about making money or having things, eventually you will burn out or get to the point where you have enough. I want to encourage you to build a mindset and culture in your business of helping people. If you make it about helping and lifting others and making a difference in their lives, then you will never burn out or even plateau for long.

Work, in general, can bring you more happiness. Have you ever noticed lazy people complain a lot? They are not as happy. Work brings a feeling of accomplishment. It's feeling gratification about your effort and yourself. A job well-done improves your self-esteem and self-discipline, which helps to close the gap I mentioned earlier.

Take my middle son, Austin, for example. He is the sporty and sometimes messy one, leaving trash, snacks, shoes, and baseball or football gear around my house daily. He only keeps his bedroom floor clear so his "roommate" and best friend, a pug dog named Fluffy, doesn't chew anything up. His room always has a lingering smell. It's like a combination of steamy athletic gear, dirty socks, and dog breath.

Once in a while, he will get the idea to do a full cleaning in there. I guess it gets to the point where it's even too much for him to bear. He will spend hours cleaning his room and organizing his closet and dusting his shelves. Garbage bags full of trash and old toys, marbles, and other random junk will be hauled out to the trash. He will even vacuum and set up his sports awards on display. Finally, when he's done, he'll call me over. Head held high, he's so proud of his work.

"Mom! Come in here! Come look at what I did in my closet! Check out under my bed."

He never got this excited over chores or jobs I gave him money for. He wasn't earning anything for this; I didn't even ask him to do it. When we work hard and do a good job, we are just happier. I loved, as a mom, the look on my son's face as he ran around his room showing me his clean nooks and crannies.

"I even made a space for Fluffy's toys to be organized! He's going to love it," he boasted.

To some, work is drudgery. They only see the grind of it. To others, it is an exciting part of life. Our attitude toward work is so important to our happiness. There is an old story where three workers in a rock quarry were asked what they were doing. One said, "Cutting rock." Another said, "Breaking my back for a crappy salary." The third worker replied with a smile, "Helping a family to build a beautiful home." The happiest people learn to enjoy work. Without work, we can't appreciate the rest and relaxation. Play and fun have less meaning. Working also helps us to improve our talents and our ability to serve our families and others. Remember, the only time success comes before work is in the dictionary. Work is a key to having full joy in this life.

I'm excited to soon cover the chapter on balance. At the same time, don't let "work-life balance" be an excuse to not put in the hard work it takes to win. You would be robbing yourself of the victory and of the happiness it will bring into your life. Make a big commitment to yourself and start taking massive action toward your vision. Ready or not, just start putting in the work. Lack of action and work will bring about doubt. Just start moving and working and your confidence will grow. Your courage and belief will continue growing. So be busy. I want to always find myself eagerly engaged in a good cause. Idleness is my enemy.

It's easy to look at a champion and see only who they are today. Don't be fooled. It was a long process to become the person they are now. Never let their victories overshadow the commitment to hard work that got them there. There is definitely an abundance of idleness in today's world. Most people will say, "It's too hard" or "I want it now; I don't want to wait that long." They constantly are asking themselves if the price is too high and if it is worth it. You can beat most of your competition just by working hard. Besides the work ethic, you'll also need grit. Grit means you have courage and show strength in your character. You stand for something. It also means you don't give up. Grit is the driver of *all* achievement. It trumps talent and brains and even short-lived intensity. It means you have perseverance to set a goal and follow through no matter what happens. You are willing to run the marathon, not just a sprint. You have the resilience to bounce back and keep going no matter what gets in your way. If you have grit, you are more consistent than your competition. As easy as that may sound, sometimes the thing that separates the people who win in life and those who don't is pure determination and *grit*! I love the great quote from Vince Lombardi, "Winning isn't everything, but wanting to win is."

Sometimes the thing that separates the people who win in life and those who don't is pure determination and grit!

Do you have stick-to-itivness (one of my favorite words)? It means dogged perseverance! Long-term tenacity! This is how you build a dream life and a legacy. I want you to ask yourself one last question before we move on.

What would it take for you to quit on your dream?

What would have to happen for you to say, "This is enough, it's not worth it"? Maybe if you went in debt or had major health challenges? Maybe if every one of your family and friends thought you were crazy, and they were all talking smack about you? What would make you give up? How about if you worked a year with no pay? Shawn went a year while sleeping in his car before he ever made a dime in business. I worked nine months without getting paid. Do you have enough faith to wait that long? Knowing what I know now, I would have waited as long as it took.

A long time ago, someone asked me, "What would make you quit?" When you get to the point that the answer to this question is "nothing," then you are gritty and ready for the big time! You have to have a made-up mind that you will never ever give up. You are in it for the long haul and will work to win. Your dream has to be so compelling to you that you are willing to do anything and everything to make it happen. Like Jeff Bezos says, "Work hard, have fun, make history."

Alright, alright. Enough with the hard, workaholic grind. But before you move on to a more exciting topic, take a few minutes to complete the following action step.

ACTION STEP

Write down all the things that would make YOU quit.

_____

_____

_____

_____

_____

_____

_____

_____

_____

_____

_____

_____

_____

9

BECOMING A LEADER

*Leadership is not about titles, positions, or flowcharts.
It is about one life influencing another.*

JOHN C. MAXWELL

I have no problem working hard. I just didn't want to work hard
forever. The idea was "pay now, play later." My next step was to
build a business that I didn't need to be present in all the time. I
come across so many people who think they own a business, but
in reality, the business owns them. They work morning until night
running every aspect of their company. I didn't want to have to
always be working *in* my business, so I had to start thinking like
an entrepreneur and work *on* my business. I wanted to learn how
to create systems to run my company and create more lifestyle for
myself. Does this sound like something you want as well? More
lifestyle, time with family, and freedom to travel?

I needed to grow a team. I had to develop others that I could trust to delegate to. I had to duplicate myself. Now, from the health club, I had already learned to manage people. I learned the corporate world way of getting people to perform. However, management and leadership are two very different things. Leadership is inspiring people to do more than they would have ever been able to do on their own. Leadership helps others become better, and in turn the whole company rises to a new level. I needed to become a leader. Because I was so intense, I made a million mistakes. I hurt people's feelings when I tried to challenge them. I was always micromanaging their activity. Worst of all, I would constantly show my frustration with their results. Wow, was there room for growth in this area! Becoming absolutely positive and having a great attitude was my first challenge. No one wants to follow a negative cry baby. People don't like being bossed around or managed, and they are not going to follow someone who is critiquing their every move. Working on my mentality and what came out of my mouth was a daily task. The best leaders were, first, the best followers. My goal was to become incredibly coachable and teachable. I wanted to be the best example of a team player for others and be someone worth following. I started devouring books on leadership and spending time with people I considered "vision stretchers." These are leaders who inspired me to dream even bigger. I sought out all the people in my industry that were the best at developing leaders. I studied great mentors and coaches from throughout history and the best modern-day business leaders. My little team and I would watch videos by John Maxwell on teamwork at our Monday morning meetings. Eventually, I started to ask myself questions like, "What is it like for the people who work with me? What else can I do to work on myself? How can I teach and train in a way that will inspire them to serve others?"

The best investment you can make in yourself is developing yourself as a leader. A leader is not just someone who has a title or experience. The honor of being a leader has to be *earned*. You have to earn the right to have influence in someone's life. You must first work on yourself to become someone worth following.

The great Nelson Mandela said, "I stand here before you not as a prophet, but as a humble servant of you, the people." *Leaders are servants!* This is probably one of the more important lines of this whole book. Leaders are servants! A leader is humble and has a teachable spirit. They are not selfish. The decisions leaders make are always what is best for their people. That's a lot different than a manager's mentality. He is only thinking about what is best for the company. I had to master this new mindset. My team had to come first.

Leadership is inspiring people to do more than they would have ever been able to do on their own.

Everything I did from then on was to help them grow. It really is a different thought process. I started to truly value people. I learned that I could be intense yet also nurturing and caring at the same time. I had to start to believe more in them, and they had to feel it from me. Believing in your people and who they are becoming is something all great leaders have the ability to do. I constantly work on my character to always earn the trust of my people. Remember, character is not about intelligence; it's about making the right choices. My people had to see me consistently make choices that were in their best interest. They had to see I was the same person at work, at home, and in every area of my life. More importantly, they had to know I had their back. To build a great company that produces an amazing lifestyle, you need good people. You will never retain the right people if you are a horrible leader. Put your ego away. No one likes to follow someone who is full of himself. Leaders with out-of-control egos are never as good as they think they are. Just remember, no one is irreplaceable. I'm not saying don't be confident. I'm saying if your ego gets too big, people will stop thinking you care about them.

You need to be authentic.

Sometimes leaders feel that if they let their guard down and are authentic, then they may lose credibility. They think if they aren't perfect and their team sees that, the team may not follow them. Don't worry about making mistakes. No one is flawless. There is no such thing as a perfect leader. It's OK to be the real you; they want to follow someone they can believe in. Learn the "team over me" mentality. You win when they win. I measure my success by the success of my people. If you are the only one winning, you already lost. Get to know them! Get to know their goals, their most important whys, even get to know their spouse and kids. Make yourself accessible. You are never too busy or too exclusive to help your people when they need you. Help them to progress and become happier. Instead of them just working with you and making a living, really create a relationship that serves them. When they follow you and apply what you teach them, their life should improve in some way.

There is no such thing as a perfect leader.

I think of it as making deposits in people. It's like they have an emotional bank account that you fill to truly build a relationship of trust. Every time you help them in some way, you make a deposit. Each time you show them that you are honest and trustworthy, it's another deposit. Every time you recognize them for their efforts or give them a kind encouragement, another deposit. When you overlook their mistakes and forgive, you make huge deposits. These deposits accumulate slowly overtime. However, withdrawals happen quickly or even all at once. If you mistreat someone or break their trust, it's an automatic full withdrawal. One of our biggest core values in my company is simply to *treat people right*. Treat them fairly and respectfully. As a leader, there is absolutely no place for prejudice. Their rewards are purely based on their performance, not on their sex, race, or anything else. Learn to love people. Your team is truly your most valuable asset.

Look for your teammates' strengths and ignore their weaknesses. Again, people need someone to believe in them. Everyone has positive qualities. Some may be harder to notice at first, but they are there. It's your job as a leader to figure out what those strengths are and build on them. When you figure out their unique talents and strengths, make sure you tell them what you see. People love it when you notice their natural gifts and abilities. This also helps them believe in themselves.

Just like you and me, most people have a hard time believing in themselves at first. They have to borrow *your* belief in them, for a little while, until their confidence has grown. Years ago, there was a young lady I coached who got started in business for herself and was so excited. She got off to a fast start and was growing quickly. After a few months of my mentoring her, she was ready to do everything on her own. One Thursday afternoon, she called me pretty upset. She was disappointed in the outcome of an appointment she had with a client. In tears and ready to give up, she went on and on about how bad she was at the business.

After listening to her cry about how she wasn't good enough and how she was letting me down, I asked her the details of this appointment she had. I reassured her that I would have had the same outcome and that she did nothing wrong. We had a great talk about how I knew she would be one of the biggest success stories in my business. I told her how talented I thought she was. I told her that the business was built for women like her and that she would change thousands of lives. We talked about how great it was going to feel because she would be the hero to her children. I reminded her of how she would become the go-to person in her family and be able to retire her parents. I told her I had never worked with someone as good as her, and I knew that she could do this. Everything I told her that night was true. Today she makes over half a million a year and has changed the lives of so many of her clients and colleagues. She just needed to be reassured by someone who believed in her.

Over and over again, tell them why they will win and what it is that you see that is so special. It could be that they are great at promoting events or that they are an amazing communicator. Maybe they have grit and tenacity. It could be their strength of character. It could be how organized and structured they are. Again, everyone has something to build on. When you point out the weaknesses they possess, you become just like the boss they didn't like or the teacher in high school they hated. They obviously know their weaknesses. Ignore that and build the person to become better and happier. He or she will develop and be more productive.

It's not just recognizing the strengths though. It's recognition for every little thing. A corporate manager usually only recognizes people when they do something wrong. You get "written up" or even demoted. I worked at that corporate gym job for almost four years without a single vacation. I never asked for a sick day or came in late. Actually, I often worked more hours than I was paid for. I found out how much the managers really cared about me when I called in sick one spring day.

I was working at the Encino location, and I was dating a guy whose little brother had been involved in a motorcycle accident. He was only nineteen and had died instantly. Of course, I wanted to be there for my boyfriend and thought missing one day wouldn't hurt anything. It didn't; my assistant and staff did fine without me on that Saturday. But on Monday morning, my corporate manager was there waiting for me.

Again, I will change her name here. Let's call her Tammy. She was a mean-spirited woman in her early sixties. She had a thin, fit body and looked like she'd been on one of those Stairmaster cardio machines every day since the '80s. Have you ever known an older female who dresses sexy, acts twenty, and is overly aggressive to any young, cute girl? That was Tammy.

As soon as I clocked in, she grabbed my arm and hissed, "In your office, now." She slammed the door, sat at my desk in my chair, and said, "Sit!" She then started screaming so loudly that everyone in all the offices could hear her perfectly.

A leader strives to find ways to always encourage, praise, and recognize. A manager discourages, intimidates, and puts you down.

"You will pay for this! I'm going to hit you in the pocketbook!" She went on and on like a lunatic. It was so absurd to get this upset because an employee called in sick. Especially since this was the only time I missed a day of work in almost four years.

"You will get walk-in sales last and no bonuses the rest of the month!" she screamed. All I could think about was how she never once asked if I was OK or how I was feeling. She never found out about the death of that nineteen-year-old boy, and I didn't dare ask for a day off to attend the funeral. It was the only time I had ever called in sick. That one day was enough to empty my emotional bank account with her forever. A leader strives to find ways to always encourage, praise, and recognize. A manager discourages, intimidates, and puts you down. Encourage people when they are struggling. Even your best guys will sometimes go into a slump.

Hold their hand and help them get back on track. Praise them when they do something right. It could be as simple as a "good job" or a fist bump. It could just be acknowledging their efforts. They could do something that might be super easy for you to do, but for them, it took a lot of courage.

They deserve to be praised.

People tend to repeat the things they did to receive recognition. Work hard to find reasons to celebrate all wins. Encourage, praise, and recognize them regardless of your feelings. You could be annoyed at them for something else but praise them for what they did right and do it fast. If you have a victory, give your people the credit for it. Every milestone in their career, make a huge deal out of it. Give out awards and trophies and do it publicly whenever possible. This doesn't have to cost you a ton of money; just make it fun and meaningful.

I once had a woman come up to me and tell me that I had changed her life. She told me a story of how I had given her a pin in a meeting in front of a large audience and had said how much I believed in her. I honestly didn't remember that pin or the night she was referring to. As I tried to recall what she was talking about, she pulled a small button-sized lapel pin out of her purse. It was yellow and had a red star on it. I had picked up a few of them at a Party City for ten cents each and gave them out one night to a few "up-and-comers." I talked about how they were rising stars. Can you believe a ten-cent award could completely change this woman's whole future? That's the power of sincere recognition. I've given out dream trips, but I have also given out simple, silly awards. One of my favorite awards was when I gave out a box of laundry detergent, a broom, and a big sponge. The person whom I was recognizing was number one that month in almost every category. I called it the "You Cleaned House" award. The whole team had fun with it, and it stirred up some healthy competition. Just don't be fake when praising and recognizing individuals.

You have to be as sincere as possible with this. I once had a guy on my team who would praise people by doing that cheesy hand gesture where you put the two fingers up like guns pointing at them. He would say, "Heeeeey champion!" So corny. People could feel his ego and knew he only cared about himself.

Remember that the reason you are becoming a leader is to raise up other independent leaders. You want to create more lifestyle. Having a team gives you the freedom from having to work in your business all the time to keep it going. The goal is to get others to buy in to your vision and help you fulfill it. Simply put, you can't be a jerk. Would you want to follow someone who doesn't appreciate your efforts?

There are three steps to building a leader:
1. Build a quality relationship.
2. Give great instruction.
3. Challenge them.

First, you must take the time to build a real relationship. You must build trust. This takes you investing a good amount of your time in them. Meet with them often; face to face is best. Have them over to your house if possible. If face to face isn't an option, over the phone or a virtual meeting would be my next choice. Just remember that email, text, and DMs are for information, not inspiration. They are a lower form of communication that doesn't build people up. Building a quality, trusting relationship takes time, and it takes you consistently adding deposits into their life.

The second step to building a leader is giving quality instruction. Teach people how to win. I'm sure you have heard that old saying, "People don't care how much you know until they know how much you care." This is why taking the time to build a relationship is so important. Make sure you continually give feedback and guidance until they are able to do it on their own. Never abandon them.

And third, challenge them. You could challenge them to do more or perform on a higher level. It could also be challenging the way they think. Some leaders have no problem challenging people, but if there is no relationship built, it may not work. If they know that you are challenging them because you care about them and believe in them, they will move and perform at a new level.

Once I had learned these basic principles of becoming a leader and building others, I had to work on my business system and on the culture in my company. This means simplifying every aspect of the business to the point where anyone can do it. I wanted to be able to train people faster, and I wanted the people I trained to be able to teach any future teammates. I created an SOP (Standard Operating Procedure) for everything. If I hired a new assistant, there was a manual that taught them everything. This will free you to do bigger projects.

Think about your business. Go through each aspect of your work. Ask yourself, *Is there a way to simplify this? Can I get the same result with less words so others can learn it faster?* Break each major area of your business into five or six steps max. If possible, create simple flip charts or PowerPoint presentations that can do the teaching for you. I focused on creating a machine. All I had to do was make sure it was running smoothly. I drove the activity and added the passion, but *a system* runs my business. Now I can travel the world, be at all my kids' games, and my business just keeps growing. I still go through periodically and tighten up the subsystems, looking for ways to simplify them and make them run even faster.

Last, I focused on the environment and culture I wanted to build. I wanted resourcefulness, positivity, and a culture of teamwork. I squashed gossiping immediately and taught people to deal direct if they had a problem with someone. Otherwise, they had to "Let it goooo!"

Foster an environment where there is always a common team goal but people can have their own big goals within that vision. I want an environment where people feel they can speak up. You don't want a bunch of yes-men and yes-women who kiss your butt all the time. You want a mastermind team who will work collaboratively; create new, better ideas; and do what is best for the overall company. All decisions should be win-win. Speaking of yes-men, years ago one of the ladies on my leadership team, Ericka, kept telling me I had to dress better. Back then I was so focused on the growth of the company that I didn't waste any time on things like shopping or getting my nails done. Most days I just showered, threw on clothes, and quickly put my hair back in a ponytail. Ericka would say, "Jaime, you're a CEO, girl! You have to start to look like one, Baby Cakes." (She always calls people she loves Baby Cakes or Boo.)

As long as there is the intention to lift others and help the whole team, conflict creates meaningful change.

One afternoon, Ericka and another great friend and teammate named Jazmin took all my hair scrunchies out of my drawer. Jazmin even took the ugly gray scrunchie I was wearing at the time. I sat there at my desk with a weird bump in my hair that was left behind from the ponytail they had removed. I think they even threatened to burn the scrunchies and a few of my oversized suits. We all laughed, and in the end, they agreed to give me back one of the scrunchies as long as I agreed I would only wear it for the rest of the day and never again after that. Could you imagine a conversation like this in a corporate setting? Not at all. I wasn't building yes-men; I was building leaders. Just know if you plan on raising up leaders, they are going to have opinions. We joke, have fun, call each other out, and sometimes have conflict. Conflict can be a great thing if done right. As long as there is the intention to lift others and help the whole team, conflict creates meaningful change.

The leaders in my group came up with a collective set of rules and values that we all believe make us stronger. We call it our Code of Honor. Most of the principles of its creation we learned in a book by Blair Singer called *The ABCs of Building a Business Team That Wins*. Our Code of Honor keeps us all working together as a cohesive team, playing from the same set of rules, and even calling one another out once in a while in a supportive way.

I achieved some of my biggest goals and dreams. I have built an amazing life, but it was because of the unbelievable team I surrounded myself with. They have selflessly served one another for years and have proved the philosophy of "Team Over Me" is profitable and fun. They have inspired me and kept me wanting to always become a better person and leader.

There is truth to this beautiful quote: "To be a member of a championship team is a great honor, but to be the leader of a championship team is one of the greatest rewards in life." Even if you are passionate about what you do, you don't want your business to own you. Learn to lead so you can gain freedom from your work. The more people you help to find success, the more successful you will become as well.

Now you know more of who I am and where I came from. I've shared with you a little of my philosophy in business and how I got to where I am today. Again, many people have become successful in business; that's not really the reason you are reading this book. You want to know how to do it and have happiness, balance, and fulfillment while chasing your biggest dreams. Let's move into how to build a Happy & Strong life.

But first, complete the following action step for this chapter.

ACTION STEP

Write down your strengths, and if you have a partner, their strengths as well. If you don't have a partner, do this with your best friend. Then share with each other what you wrote. (Extra credit: Write down all the unique talents and gifts of your children and share it with them.)

_____

_____

_____

_____

_____

_____

_____

_____

_____

_____

10

Make Your Priorities a Priority!

If you want to change the world, go home and love your family.

Mother Theresa

Finally. The chapters that you have been waiting for are here. By now, you're thinking, "It's about time, Jaime. Just tell me how to manage it all before I lose my mind."

I speak all over the country at live events and now virtually as well. I've spoken for very small groups and groups as large as 60,000. I love mentoring and coaching; it's one of my favorite parts of what I do. I'm so passionate about helping others find happiness, balance, and fulfillment while still chasing their biggest goals and dreams.

The question I get most often as I travel is, "How do you do it, Jaime? How do you do it with kids and trying to juggle it all?" Well, I am always busy. But like I said, I like busy. I don't have any desire to be average and ordinary. I'm not one to veg out and do nothing. At least not very often. My schedule can be full sometimes, but the question is, full of what? Kids, work, church and charity, time with your spouse . . . is there such a thing as too much of a good thing? I really do believe the answer is yes. Being busy and happy is fine. Busy and stressed, overworked, and miserable is not. Let's talk first about priorities, then we can get into self-care, health, and other good stuff.

"The greatest work you will ever do will be within the walls of your home."
—Harold B. Lee

You can't have too many priorities. You already know mine: faith, family, fitness, and finances (or business)—in that order. Again, what's the point of being rich and successful if your kids hate you and you are divorced or emotionally bankrupt? That is not happiness! I don't want you to be rich in the wallet but poor at home.

One of my favorite quotes is from Harold B. Lee. I have it on a family photo in my dining room. He said, "The greatest work you will ever do will be within the walls of your home." It's a great reminder of what's most important.

I knew a man who was a super wealthy bachelor, had a big house in Hollywood Hills, and had many girlfriends. He had built the dream life he imagined. Yet he was not fulfilled. He was on depression medicine and told me he had no "real" friends. His first wife hated him, and his kids rarely spoke to him. He wondered if he would ever have another meaningful relationship. He worried the girls he was dating just wanted him for his money. He bought art, cars, and other material things but was still unhappy.

Do you know anyone like this? They just don't know how to be happy.

Relationships are one of the keys to happiness. I mean *real* relationships, meaningful ones, not just people who like a post you made on social media. Some people have no problem with this; they love people, love socializing. Others, not so much. Maybe you're an introvert or too busy to invest a lot of time into nurturing a friendship. You might be thinking, "I barely have enough time to take care of my kids and myself right now, Jaime." Happy people have good friends and relationships. Maybe you don't have a ton of really close friends, and that's perfectly fine, but take time to be a friend to those you do have.

If you are married, the most important relationship is with your spouse. If you're not married yet, choose wisely when you do decide on "the one." One key to a wonderful, happy life is a quality marriage. A spouse can make or break you in business. I've seen it a thousand times. Your marriage must be a top priority, putting it even before the kids. Do you have regular date nights? Make sure that date nights are a priority in your house. Everyone I do business coaching for has to do date nights with their spouse. You have heard "happy wife, happy life." Well also, happy husband, happy life. Happy spouse, happy kids! Make sure you take that time to reconnect and keep courting each other.

Dating your spouse helps you keep your love life sizzling hot and breeds happiness into your whole household. It's good for the kids to see their parents wanting to be together and that they make each other a priority. So many times, couples are too scared to leave their kids with a babysitter, so they never get to go out for a night alone or a romantic getaway. I don't want to be dismissive of a real fear that you may have, but this can be hurtful to a marriage. I know that it's hard to find someone you trust to leave your kids with, but maybe start small by being gone for only an hour or less. I choose not to live in fear and have found some amazing sitters over the years who have loved my children.

If you don't have family you trust nearby, ask for some good referrals from ladies you trust at church or your circle of friends. It is healthy for the kids, your spouse, your love life, and your state of happiness to get some time alone away from the kids. Pick a time weekly (or biweekly as a worst-case scenario) for regular date nights.

Shawn and I also have "partnership meetings." We are true partners in life, parenting, and business. Neither one of us makes the other do any particular role or bosses the other around. (OK, I can get a little bossy, but I don't mean to be.) And there may be the occasional role playing, but I digress.

If you are married, understand that your spouse can be your secret weapon in business. I'm really grateful for how much Shawn does in our partnership, and I know he appreciates me as well. Show that respect and appreciation to your partner. Our partnership meetings are usually short. We go over our goals or schedules. We talk about any issues with the business, the household, or the kids. We plan our next adventures and try to show support for each other's ideas. Sunday night when the kids are in bed is usually a great time to do this. It's a peaceful time in my home, and Shawn and I are not distracted with the cares of the outside world. Our life and our marriage take priority at that moment. Remember, the goal is to be on the same page, a team. Two people working toward a common goal is so powerful; it's more like ten individuals.

Let me stop and give you a few tips on what *not* to do if you are in business with your spouse, especially if you want more support from them. I coached a guy in business who does extremely well and is in the top 1 percent of income earners now in the world. He started with me, young and single and hating his job, looking to have his own business. When he finally met a girl he liked and wanted me to meet her, he was so excited.

"Jaime, make her want to do the business with me."

"I can't make anyone do anything," I laughed. He really wanted me to sell her on the dream of being in business with her spouse so she would want to quit her job and help him. It was so cute (and a little creepy).

Another guy I coached had his wife on payroll and was making her do all his follow-up calls. That's fine if she wants to help in that area, but she didn't like doing it, to say the least. She ended up quitting and getting a job somewhere else. At least she didn't quit on the marriage.

Your spouse can't be your employee; they are your *partner*. You can't force your partner to get on the same page with you. After helping so many couples in this situation, here is the best advice I can give: Instead of trying to figure out your roles or divvying up responsibilities between the two of you, sit down together and create your common vision. Practice dreaming together. You can go somewhere nice and relaxing like the beach, or you can just sit on your bed with a legal pad on your lap like Shawn and I have done countless times.

At the end of this chapter, you'll take some time to create your bucket list dreams. Throw out ideas, wishes, and fun lifestyle dreams. Don't be negative if your spouse wants something you don't. That's OK. Shawn has wanted huge fifteen-car garages and old hot rod classic cars. I don't have any interest in those things, but I love that he is dreaming big, so I write it down. Talk about your ideal life, what you want for your kids and your parents. Get on the same page about values and parenting. Don't forget contribution goals, charity, and the dream home. Just have fun with it.

Once you have a common vision for your future big enough to fit all the dreams that you both want individually and as a couple, you are ready. When you have a shared vision for the family and life that you are building *together* that both of you are excited about, you won't have to figure out who does what and your individual roles. You will work as partners, filling the needs of what's next. Sometimes Shawn cooks or does the dishes. Sometimes it's me. We pick up whatever needs to get done and roll with it. He does stuff at the kids' school; so do I. Appreciation and communication with your spouse is such a big part of winning in business and in marriage. A happy marriage contributes to a happy life.

> *The best thing you can do for your kids is give them an example of a happy relationship with your spouse.*

Make your spouse number one, even before your kids. It may sound harsh or uncomfortable for some of you because your kids are your whole world. But think about it—the best thing you can do for your kids is give them an example of a happy relationship with your spouse. You are modeling for them how to be happy. Don't you wish for them to grow up and marry the man or woman of their dreams and live a life with a fulfilling, passionate marriage? Of course you do; you want the best for your children. Remember the incredible quote from Theodore Hesburgh, "The most important thing a father can do for his children is love their mother."

Balancing a career and kids can be challenging. Mommy guilt is real. It's not just moms though; I have talked to so many dads who feel the same way.

When you are at the office or working, you may feel that you are spending too much time away from home. In contrast, when you are home a lot, you may feel like you are neglecting your business. This happened to me when Daisy, my first baby, was about eighteen months old. If you don't have kids or don't plan on having kids, you won't hurt my feelings if you skip ahead to page 143.

For the first time in my career, I was seriously distracted. Mommy guilt! Up until that point, I loved what I did. When Shawn and I decided it was time to start having kids, some people discouraged us. They said it would hurt our income and company. Ridiculous! I decided a long time ago that family would always come first. If we couldn't run our business or our income went down because of our kids, we were both OK with that.

Deciding when to start a family is a personal decision between you and your partner. However, let me just say that you shouldn't let where you are in your career be the deciding factor. I know that's not usually what you will hear. Many "power women" and "boss-babes" say they put off having kids to forward their growth in business. Not me. That is too high of a price for success. The reason you are reading this book is to learn "how to have it all!" Kids are probably the most rewarding part of "it all," so when you feel it's time to start your family, go ahead. Don't stress. You will learn to increase your capacity, and it will all work out.

Throughout my pregnancy, I still worked. It wasn't like I was doing manual labor; besides, my work brings me joy, so I didn't feel the need to slow down. Shawn said I was even making phone calls to help people while at the hospital in labor.

Let's flash back to the mommy guilt that started when Daisy was about a year and a half old. (If you have kids, this has probably been on your mind at some point.)

Daisy went everywhere with us, including the office. I had a swing and Pack 'n Play there, and she had dozens of "aunties and uncles" happily waiting for a chance to hold her when I did an appointment. I held her in my arms as I delivered a training message to hundreds of people in Anaheim. She slept quietly in Ed Mylett's office as we strategized with him about how to get to our next level in business. I loved being able to have my kids around as I worked. We were building a family business, and we loved it.

That's why I wasn't expecting the mommy guilt. I didn't even recognize it when it started. Daisy was a little bigger and couldn't just take naps at the office anymore. I had to get a babysitter sometimes. At first, I just felt uneasy. I started asking myself things like, "Is it worth it?" It was especially bad when I had to do a late night appointment. I would get home and she was already in bed.

Mommy/parent guilt is real and it's a big distraction. I couldn't give it 100 percent when I was at work or when I was at home. As much as I love what I do, I love my family so much more, and I was growing unhappy. I felt a little like I was fake and going through the motions. It went on like this for about a month, and finally I had to make changes.

Like in business when I am stuck, I called a mentor. I told him how I was feeling, and he suggested Shawn and I come out to visit him and his wife.

Rich and Cindy Thawley are the best example of Happy & Strong that I know, successful beyond measure in every area of their lives. They are incredibly wealthy yet humble and generous. They have a world-class marriage and strong family bonds with their three children and grandchildren. They are servants in their community and church. This amazing couple had already been through what I was going through, and I needed guidance. We immediately accepted the invitation and went to see them in Northern California. We had a great talk and felt loved with no judgment at all. They told us some stories of when they were in our shoes and then put it back on us to decide what's best for our family.

Rich gave me some loving fatherly advice.

"You can quit the business and do something else entirely. Or you can take a step back, Jaime, and just let Shawn run it while you stay home with the baby," he said. "*Or* you can figure out a new way to do what you want to do so you feel good about it again."

A new way? This is what balance is: figuring out what works for you right now. Rich told me to pray about it, and Shawn and I left there feeling excited again.

A new way was exactly what I needed. As soon as I was back home, I sat down with my legal pad and wrote out a new schedule I could feel good about. I created a daily schedule that worked both for Shawn and me. I made sure to schedule in my family time first. I carved out time alone with Shawn to reconnect and plenty of time with my daughter. Then I put in the main things about what I love to do in my business. I identified the activities that could be delegated. I even discovered some that I did *not* need to do but still hadn't applied the "Let it goooo!" technique yet.

The next day, I tried to rigidly stick to my new way of doing things. Yeah, that didn't work. But over the next few weeks, I kept tweaking it and adjusting it until finally that mommy guilt was gone. You will know you are on the right track when you have a feeling of peace again. I maxed out when I was working, and I maxed out during family time. I had never felt more fulfilled.

When I had my second child, it was like throwing another log on the fire. Not a big deal; two wasn't much harder than one. Austin was my second child, and he was the most precious chubby, sweet little chunkers ever. As I would look into his adorable, innocent eyes or stare at him as he slept next to me in my bed, I fell so in love with him. He made me want another baby right away. As the result of his irresistible charm, I got pregnant with Brody only nine months after having Austin.

Now, three is a whole other deal. Three is the hardest. Side note, if you are going to have three, you might as well go for number four. It's actually easier. Three is rough. Not that Brody was a hard baby; he's actually my easiest child. But with three, you are outnumbered.

Mommy guilt started creeping in again, and it was back to the drawing board. I tweaked and adjusted things until I was comfortable, happy, and at peace again. This is how you balance; it's different for each of us. And just to let you in on a secret, there is no such thing as perfect balance, only striving for balance and happiness.

Let me give you a couple of pointers on how I have managed work-life balance. I've done millions of tweaks and adjustments. It's been an evolving plan with so many changes and compromises after having four children.

First is mommy dates. Schedule time with each individual child. These don't have to be expensive. They can just be doing something like going to get milkshakes. I try to spend time with each of them individually, figuring out what they are into and how school is going and discovering any new talents or passions. These mommy (and daddy) dates can be as often as you feel necessary, but do it at least once every month.

There is no such thing as perfect balance, only striving for balance and happiness.

On top of these mommy dates, every day I try to spend at least ten minutes of one-on-one time with each child. Our daily lives can get so busy. It's important to make time for undivided, meaningful attention with no distractions, no siblings, and no cell phone, even if it's just for ten minutes. That may not seem like much, but a lot of days we go way over. It could be as simple as reading a book at bedtime. With four kids (and all their activities), sometimes ten minutes can be a hard thing to do. I also schedule family days so we can get the much-needed family time all together. Again, this doesn't have to be expensive. It can be a hike, a beach day, or a bike ride. Some of our favorite family days didn't cost anything at all.

Sundays are super important to our family. We don't schedule any work activities or allow our kids to do sports that are scheduled on Sundays. This one day is set aside for church and family time. I highly recommend that you have a certain time every week that the whole family can look forward to so you have special family time together. This is Sundays for us; we play board games or watch uplifting movies, have a picnic outside, or just lay around the house being restful. We all love and look forward to our Sunday together. No homework, no one is calling my phone, just peaceful family togetherness.

I don't believe in overscheduling kids, or myself for that matter. So many parents feel that their kids need to be involved in different activities all the time, as if their kids will not be well-rounded if they're not in karate, dance, and a million other things. Maybe they are trying to give their children the life they never had and live vicariously through them. I definitely do not relish the idea of being a taxi driver, driving to kids' events every day. My kids are in one activity at a time, but you can imagine with four kids that's still a lot of driving around.

Besides that, overscheduled kids tend to be more stressed out. And I know for sure *I* would be more stressed out. My kids know I love them, but they also know that their father and I are a team and on the same page with the common vision of a happy family. My goal in life is not to entertain my kids. Why do Americans feel they have to constantly keep their kids busy? Organizing playdates, putting them in camps, and endless extra-curricular activities— it's like parents are their children's personal assistants. I believe in letting them play outside and even be bored once in a while. Let them become resourceful and figure out how to entertain them-selves. Kids need to learn how to create their own happiness too.

Don't get me wrong, all my kids are doing lots of fun clubs and activities. I'm just careful that they are not so busy that it's disrup-tive to the family unit. They have done everything from sports, guitar, drums, viola, and trumpet. (Oh, the trumpet. That was my least favorite.) They have church activities, Scouts, art, drama, choir, martial arts, coding, horse camps, baking classes, and volunteer work. I love watching them develop their talents and discover who they are and what they love, but I won't do it at the expense of our time together as a family. My rule is one thing at a time and not on Sundays.

You might have another day that works better for your family. Sunday has always worked out well for ours. There have been a few times when the kids asked to go to a birthday party on a Sunday or join a sport that plays on Sundays, and we have to talk about it. So far, we have kept that day as our sacred family time, and I know we have been blessed because of it.

People always ask if it will get easier when the kids get older. Nope! It will just be different. Babies are a lot of work; toddlers are a different kind of difficult. Grade-schoolers have all the activities and events you have to learn to balance into your schedule. And teenagers…well that's a whole new stage of personal development you get to go through.

I love each of these stages, even the teenager stage. Just remember, it's hard to adjust and balance if you are overly involved. What I mean by that is I am involved in every area of my kids' lives, but I can't live it for them. They need to make their own choices and mistakes. I see some parents doing their kids' homework for them. *Are you kidding?* Or buttoning their eight-year-old's pants. *What?* Now if your child is special needs, of course there are exceptions, but most parents just have to let kids do things on their own. To all you helicopter parents, "Let it goooo! Let it goooo!" If they can do it on their own, let them.

For the most part, my kids do well in school. They know my job is to run the house and pay the bills. Their job is to do their best in school and help with all the household chores. Homework is part of their job, not mine. Of course, there is the occasional school project or science fair that Shawn and I will jump in and help out with, but day to day, homework is up to them. I have one son who struggles with school and another child with a learning disability, so, trust me, I know there can be some frustrating school and homework moments. One of my children has severe ADHD. Sitting all day in class is torture, just to come home to sit some more and do hours of homework. For the special cases, come up with a plan together with your spouse, child, and teacher. If the school needs to get involved, then fight for that as well. I'm just saying, don't let it turn into you being frustrated and spending countless hours of your life at the kitchen table doing schoolwork. I already went through fifth grade; I don't need to do it again. Let your child feel heard, loved, and supported, but be careful to not get sucked into the homework trap.

One of my sons is kind of a rebel. I will leave his name out to save him embarrassment. He would come home from fourth grade and say his homework was too hard, trying to sucker me into babying him. He wanted to hook me into rescuing him as he would sit there with a look of confusion on his face. This is where so many parents lose hours of their week practically doing their kids' homework for them. Maybe some parents like that time together. I would rather spend quality time in other ways.

"Really?" I would ask of him. "I thought you had a nice teacher. She's a liar. She told me she only gave out about ten minutes of homework at night. She said that it's stuff you should be able to handle. Don't do it! Put it all away and don't do that hard homework. Tomorrow during recess, go in and tell your teacher it's way too hard for you and that you need extra help. You can get extra help on it during recess." He always had his homework done in five minutes.

There have been times when one of the kids needed extra support in a subject. Shawn and I will always communicate and come up with a plan to make sure they get it. But I'm not at the kids' beck and call, and they have learned to be resourceful.

How about chores? If there is anything that can suck your time and happiness, it's nagging kids to clean up. Again, I want to raise resourceful kids, and I don't have time to chase them around telling them to take out the trash. We have a responsibility chart. Trust me, you will be thanking me for this tip. I got the idea from a great book called *Three Steps to a Strong Family* by Richard and Linda Eyre. The kids have morning, after-school, dinnertime, and bedtime responsibilities. The chart has a spot for each of these sections for each day. In the morning, they have to get themselves up and ready for school, brush their teeth, eat, and be out the door in time for school. Those are the morning responsibilities. After school, they have chores, practice, and homework to complete before they can go out to play or get on any electronics. They each have dinnertime chores and bedtime responsibilities before going to bed on time.

Build self-motivated, responsible kids. Don't do things for them that they can easily do on their own.

I don't want to be the nagging mom, and frankly I don't have time for it. My kids don't get an allowance. They earn money for the extracurricular activities and other stuff they want through this responsibility chart. If I have to remind them to do their chores, homework, or to get up in the morning, then they lose that part of their pay on payday. Build self-motivated, responsible kids. Don't do things for them that they can easily do on their own. Then the stressful things you are trying so hard to balance go away, and you are balancing fun family time and quality time that bring you more happiness. That's not too hard to do.

Let me give you an example of how this looks. Let's use Daisy. It's her responsibility to set an alarm and wake up on time. She has to eat, brush her teeth, and be ready to leave pretty early. If I have to go into her room and nag her to hurry up, she loses the credit on that part of her chart. She still has to do the chores, but if she has to be reminded, then she gets no money. After school she completes her homework, practices piano or basketball, and does her after-school chores.

These after-school chores vary. It could be cleaning the refrigerator, cleaning a certain area of the house, or their favorite, picking up the dog poop in the yard. I will tell you what it's not. It's not cleaning their room. They don't get money for that. Cleaning their room and doing their laundry are responsibilities they must keep up.

I will tell you it gets done because they can't go do the fun things they want to do with their friends if the room is a mess. One of my children, again not naming him here, has been known to wear the same pair of socks or other clothes several times to avoid doing his laundry. It can get a little gross sometimes, but that is a price I'm willing to pay.

The dinnertime chore is an easy one. Everyone in the house eats here, so everyone contributes. At dinnertime, it's a team effort. Shawn and I usually do the cooking, but the older kids will jump in once in a while. Other dinner chores could be chopping veggies, clearing the table, or loading the dishwasher. You get the picture. The bedtime responsibilities are the hardest ones, at least in my house. This means they have to brush their teeth, shower, get their pj's on, and be in bed at bedtime so I can come tuck them in. Easier said than done. It's a work in progress.

We keep a laminated responsibility chart on our refrigerator so everyone can see. It has all the kids' names and the days of the week on it. There are spaces for each of the four chores categories as well, each representing an amount of money they can earn. For example, let's say each section represents twenty-five cents. If they do their morning, afterschool, dinnertime, and bedtime chores, they will earn one dollar that day. If they did everything for the whole week, Monday through Friday, that would be five dollars. You decide how much to pay them based on their ages and how much their activities cost. They use the money on whatever they want.

At the end of each day, it is their job to initial each section they completed without being reminded. I keep a dry erase marker in the drawer near the fridge. They won't lie because that automatically makes them lose all pay for the week. I don't have to tell them what to do; I don't have to nag. The system creates so much more peace and happiness in the home, not to mention the time saved that you can spend doing more productive things. Saturday is payday. They go to Shawn wanting their money. It's their responsibility to add up how much they made, figure out how much of it they want to save, how much to tithe, and how much to keep. There have been times where one of my kids did all his chores but forgot to mark it each day. Too bad, so sad. They can't go back and fill it in later. Remember, this is not about the clean house; it's about creating a strong and happy family.

We have a family bank that they can save in, and Shawn gives them a 12 percent return a year. Pretty awesome, if you ask me. They can choose to invest here long term to buy a car or for anything else they get excited about.

When I am at the store and Daisy asks for some cute boots, I say, "Of course, you can buy whatever you want. Did you bring your wallet?" I don't buy my kids' stuff. They use their own money. Usually, she will look at the price tag of the boots and say, "What? These are way too expensive." I love it. They learn the value of money.

On Saturdays, I put up a list of things they can do for money. It could be things like picking weeds, scrubbing toilets, or scraping salt buildup off the pool. This way if they have something special they need money for, like football gear or a camp they want to attend, they have a chance to earn it.

I know you have a lot on your plate if you have little ones. This will be the hardest time in your whole life. You may have a job or business, kids, and could also be helping your aging parents. I know it's a lot, but you can do this. You will get through it. Your kids will be fine, and they will be so proud of you. As busy as you sometimes can be, just make sure you are unconditionally loving each of those babies. Each child has to know in their heart how much they are loved and adored. Tell them; show them often. Tell them that no matter what, they are the most important thing in your life:

"No matter what you do, I will never stop loving you" or "There is nothing you could ever do that would make me love you less; in fact, I will love you even more tomorrow."

My kids have often heard me say, "Dad's my favorite, but then there is nothing in the world that comes close to you. You are my treasure."

They know that the business is what we do, but it will never come before our family. However, there have been times they have tested that.

Brody might ask, "Do you really have to be gone tonight?" as I'm leaving to a work appointment. I just look at him and say, "Nope, I can stay home. I was going to go help a family."

I would tell them a little about the person or family I was going to be with that night.

"They have a little girl a little younger than you. They need some help. Should I help that family or just stay home and watch TV with you?"

Every time, they ask a few questions and then say, "You should help them."

On a hot Saturday in July, I mentioned to the kids that the team was coming over to our house for a BBQ and to swim. Daisy looked at me and said, "The team? Why? I wanted to just hang out and watch a movie marathon." This was probably during her Harry Potter phase.

A little irritated at her tone, I said, "That team bought you that pool; they bought you that big screen TV. They are coming over today and so are their kids. Don't you think you should show them how much you appreciate their hard work?" I could tell she had never thought of it that way. She just thought I was the boss. When the team got to our house that day, Daisy was the greatest little hostess. She brought out the cupcakes and was serving everyone. She even organized some fun activities for all the kids to play. This was one of the best lessons she learned about leadership. Leaders are not a boss; they are a servant. She had a lot of fun that Saturday; our whole family did. Involve your kids as much as you can. For instance, if you have a big goal you are trying to hit, get them invested.

"If Daddy hits his goal this month, each of you can get your own favorite pint of ice cream in the freezer" or "If Mommy hits the goal by the end of the month, we can go camping over the long weekend."

Get creative and have fun with it. You can also involve them by letting them be around the business. When my kids were little, we would have family days at the park with the other people in our company or with our clients. We would host charity events they could attend. Each year, we have a team Christmas party, and the kids get to stuff stockings for the local women and children's shelter. Now that Daisy is a teenager, she does data entry for me occasionally. I love that they can feel like we are building a family business.

The word "balance" makes me think of a scale where one side is always heavier than the other, opposing one another. What if, instead of family and business opposing each other, it could be more in harmony? The family is the center of everything you do; the business is just an extension of who you are and what you stand for. The main purpose of your work is to support the family, not pull away from it. When I look at it this way, instead of balancing back and forth, I am way less stressed. It allows me to focus more on my vision, and the result is way more happiness in my home.

The last thing I will add is that faith really is a priority. It helps keep you hopeful, personally growing, and progressing. The sign of a strong leader is growing closer to God. I hope this doesn't come across as offensive, but it's important to me to include. (If it does offend you, feel free to skip to the next chapter.)

The family is the center of everything you do; the business is just an extension of who you are and what you stand for.

It always felt like something was missing in my marriage and business until I made the decision to get my spiritual life together. Every single area of my life improved when I figured out what I believed in and when I started working on this one thing. I have hit some amazing, impossible goals, and I know that it wasn't all me. Another one of my favorite affirmations is, "I can do all things through Christ, who strengtheneth me."

It doesn't matter if we are not of the same faith. I coach people from every faith and religion, and I always encourage them to get their spiritual life in order. You will be happier. You will feel more peace and support. If you are an atheist and have never believed in a higher power, that's OK too. You have to start somewhere. If you don't know where to start or maybe don't really feel that the religion you grew up with is right for you, then my suggestion is to pray. Even if you don't believe, just do a little experiment and see how you feel. Pray out there to God or the Universe or whatever you feel comfortable with and just ask for help. Ask for guidance. Pour out your heart and say all that you may need help with and let Him know that you want to have a stronger spiritual life. I promise that working on this will only lead to good things. Applying faith in your life is powerful.

In 2006, Shawn and I were at the Ritz Carlton in Laguna Beach, California. It was our first CEO meeting with all the big leaders in our parent company. They took us out to a fancy dinner, and afterward we headed off to our room. Sometime in the night, I started having sharp pains in my abdomen. I was freezing and sweating and could hardly move. Shawn wanted to take me to the hospital. I decided to try to just go to sleep and see how I felt in the morning, but I couldn't sleep. I was up most of the night, shivering in agony. When morning finally came, I told Shawn to just go downstairs to the meeting without me. My plan was to get up, go to the bathroom, and then rest for a while. If I didn't feel better, I would go to the hospital.

As I walked toward the bathroom, I lost consciousness. Passing out, I fell forward completely lifeless. Thank goodness Shawn caught me right before my face crashed into the hard tile floor. Panicking, he threw cold water in my face, yelling at me to wake up. He slapped my cheeks as he watched my eyes roll back in my head. Convulsing, I lost all control of my bodily functions right there on the floor where I lay unconscious.

When I started to come to, Shawn tried to sit me up, only to make me pass out again. He laid me flat on the bed, and I finally started to come in and out of responsiveness. He cleaned me up and left me on the bed as he called for help. One of our friends came upstairs to our room to help. It was Rich Thawley, the leader I mentioned earlier who was always very caring and fatherly. He gave me a blessing, kind of like a prayer. Even though I was barely conscious, I heard some of his words. He said my body would heal itself.

Luckily, there was an on-site doctor at the Ritz, and he rushed to our room. As the doctor checked my vitals, he couldn't read my blood pressure. He couldn't even find it. He called 911, and the next thing I remember was Shawn standing outside the ambulance while they shut the door and I couldn't see him anymore. I vaguely remember two paramedics asking me questions, trying to keep me talking. Then nothing. Out again.

I woke up freezing in a hospital bed. Shawn was sitting in the corner of the room. He looked so upset. I had never seen that look of absolute fear on his face. They were running so many tests. The nurse kept bringing in warm blankets and stacking them on top of me. No matter how tall she built that wall of blankets, I shivered. There was pressure building up near my shoulder and that aching still in my abdomen. I was so weak I could barely speak. The nurses whisked me off to do a CAT scan. As I lay there in that huge white tube, I started to get really scared. *This is really serious*, I thought as I felt the hot injection come into my body. I don't remember a lot because I kept passing out, but I do remember feeling afraid.

Finally, I woke up again in the hospital bed with a nurse in my face asking me to sign documents. She informed me that they had called in a specialist vascular surgeon, and he was on the way to the hospital. I would be in emergency surgery within minutes. They just needed me to sign these papers. I looked over the documents and read that my ovaries might be removed, and they needed my permission to do so.

"What? No way! I'm not signing this!" I said adamantly as I handed her back her clipboard. I had only one baby at that point in my life, and I knew I wanted more children.

"We have no choice. Hopefully the doctor won't have to remove either of your ovaries, but you must sign this now so we can prep you for surgery. You are bleeding internally."

I sadly signed the papers, and then she quickly exited the room.

Fear and faith cannot coexist. I closed my eyes and prayed. *Heavenly Father, help me now. I know you can move a mountain. I know you can make this whole hospital crumble if you want to. This is easy. Heal me, please. This is nothing; it's so easy for you. Heal me now.*

As I pleaded and mustered up all the faith I could possibly exercise, I felt my body get warm for the first time. I felt peace and warmth all over. I opened my eyes, and there was the nurse again right in my face.

"Are you ready?" she asked.

I looked at Shawn and ran through a laundry list of things I wanted to make sure he checked on at the office and people I wanted him to call for me. He looked shocked and just shook his head as they rushed me to the operation room, and again I was out.

Shawn and others waited outside and worried while I was in surgery. It took much longer than the doctor had said. Shawn was scared. Thoughts of being a single dad came to mind. *Why is it taking so long?* he wondered. Finally, after about four or five hours, the doctor came out. In his hand were pictures from the operation.

"It's bizarre. I've been doing this for years. Exactly what we thought happened is what happened, but when we went in, her body had somehow healed itself."

He pointed to the pictures and explained what had happened less than twenty-four hours before the surgery. He pointed at the scar tissue and said he had never seen anything like this happen and had only heard of it once before. He said the surgery took so long because after cleaning out all the blood from the internal bleeding, they just kept looking to make sure there was nothing else wrong. That was it; they cleaned out the blood and sewed me back up. An absolute miracle. Faith is powerful. It healed my body, but it can also heal your heart and your home and give you strength beyond your own.

All I am saying is this one area of your life is worth improving, even if it's only in little ways. I know making my spiritual life a priority has been a huge factor in my success and in my happiness. Some ways I have made faith a priority are doing service and having self-improvement goals. I also hold personal and family prayer, engage in scripture study, and attend church regularly. A great quote and now an affirmation of mine reads, "Increasing in holiness is the only path to happiness."

> *Faith is powerful. It healed my body, but it can also heal your heart and your home and give you strength beyond your own.*

Let's apply faith to business. "Whatever the mind can conceive and believe, it can achieve." This is absolutely true. So many times in my business, I have made impossible goals happen purely because I exercised faith that it *could* happen. Faith is belief. It's believing in something that you cannot see. My friend, please understand that you exercise faith every day. You believe that when you get in your car and drive to your office you will get there just fine. You don't have to say a prayer first. You believe it without even thinking about it. This comes from experience. All those times you have entered a car since you were a little kid have proven to you that it is safe. Experience and seeing is believing. It's harder to believe something if you have no experience with it in the past.

Starting out in business, many times we are attempting something completely new to us. We have to act on faith. Even though I didn't know anyone personally who made a seven-figure income, I believed I could. The business world is filled with people who *hope* to succeed. Most don't really believe they will. They are too full of fear and doubt. They doubt they could ever build that ideal life but hope to surprise themselves and win.

Faith is a state of mind, and a state of mind can be induced. If you can make yourself believe something, then it's game over. By repeatedly reading and visualizing your goals, you create more and more belief that you will have them someday. Also, it helps to hang around people who will increase that optimism. When I am around people making five times my income, it expands my thinking. I see that these are normal people just like me. If they can do it, I can do it too.

Put yourself in positions to increase your faith regularly. For one of the action steps in this chapter, I want you to make a list of all the things you value and try to put an effort into expanding on those. My list includes things like honesty, kindness, simplicity, fun, and humor. Other values that made the list are good communication, entrepreneurialism, service, teamwork, and several others I want to make sure I'm getting better at and teaching my kids. All I am trying to say here is that faith is a huge priority in my life and one of the keys to a balanced, fulfilled, Happy & Strong life.

Our world is full of stories of people who overcame incredible odds to achieve amazing feats through faith. They believed in their abilities and that somehow their vision would come to pass. Without faith, you will automatically revert to self-doubt. We will all have our bad days. I get that. On those days, don't lose any ground. Hold strong to the vision you have for your life. Faith and fear don't exist at the same time, but you have to consciously try to increase faith and push out the doubt and failure messages. Fear eats away at your happiness and your hope. Faith is the precursor to all great accomplishments. You have to believe in yourself. The reason so many fail to realize their dream is because they don't keep pushing when doubt creeps in. *Faith diminishes fear.* It is not something to use only once in a while. It becomes like an atrophied muscle. You must keep exercising it to build the muscle of faith stronger and stronger to break new barriers. Faith will grow if you nurture it.

For now, as you work on growing a strong, unwavering faith in yourself, borrow a little of mine. Borrow my belief. I believe you have everything it takes to win at the highest levels. Maybe we haven't met yet, so there you go doubting what I am saying. Maybe you think I am overly optimistic or just trying to motivate you. No, it's my belief. You have the seed of greatness inside, and I know you can accomplish your biggest goals and dreams. If I can do it, I know you can too. I'm so excited to hear your story someday when you get there.

We will get to scheduling and time management later, but in the next chapter I'm excited to share with you my favorite affirmation and one of the biggest causes of more happiness in my life. I hope you are excited too.

Before you move on, though, take some time to complete the action steps for this chapter.

ACTION STEPS

This is a two-part action step. First, practice dreaming again. Write down some of your biggest dreams, contribution goals, and lifestyle goals. If you have a partner, do it together.

_____

_____

_____

_____

_____

_____

Second, what are your values? List them here.

_____

_____

_____

11

CREATING MEMORIES VERSUS GETTING THINGS DONE

It's realizing that a great dream is not as good as a great memory. The dream can be had by anyone. The memory must be made.

ERIC THOMAS, THE HIP-HOP PREACHER

"I love you more than anything in the world," the mom whispered, as she smiled and kissed her son on the nose.

"Even more than your phone?" his sweet little voice questioned. When I heard this story, it made me sad but it also made me wonder if my kids ever felt that way. I was always on my phone. Not texting or checking my social media. Not gossiping with a girlfriend but getting things done. Let's face it; there are always things to get done. I'm a to-do list kind of gal. I love crossing off something on my list. I'm a compulsive planner, preplanning just about everything.

Shawn makes fun of me because I even do this on vacation. We can be in Tahiti, and while he is surfing and having the time of his life, I'm happy just lying on the beach planning the next event. He is Mr. Spontaneous and fun; I'm the stick-in-the-mud who has to have an agenda for everything.

A few years ago, we went to Disneyland with some friends. When we got there and they handed me the map of the park, I immediately started to plan the whole day.

"We will start here at Adventureland, and then go up to …."

I want to enjoy my life, not just race through it.

The smiles on the kids' faces fell. They knew they were on my schedule. What a bummer.

I had never planned to be that kind of mom. Why was being efficient more important than enjoying our time together? Letting go of my need to control everything, I handed Austin the map and said, "OK, where should we go first?"

The entire day all I focused on was having fun. We wasted so much time backtracking, looking for places to eat, and waiting in unnecessary lines. It was a long day, but we had a blast. At the end of the night, I could hardly walk back to the car. I was so tired, and my feet and back were aching. Despite how worn out we all were, we had an amazing day and created some lasting memories. We got back to the hotel exhausted and *happy*.

Is it hard for you to be in the moment? It really is for me. To the point that it makes me sad sometimes. I will spend all this time planning an amazing event, family trip, or couples' getaway, and then when it comes time to do all these wonderful things I planned, my brain is already working on the next thing. No fun. I want to enjoy my life, not just race through it.

It seems I'm always rushing around and running late. If this is you, it could be a symptom of overscheduling or bad time management; either way, it's stressful. I want to empower you to live your best life. Rushing and stressing has to go. To quote Ferris Bueller, "Life moves pretty fast. If you don't stop and look around once in a while, you could miss it."

With four kids and a business, it can get hectic. I've caught myself rushing late for something and snapping at the kids, "Hurry up! Get in the car!" It's not their fault that I'm late. It's almost inevitable; every Sunday, no matter how early we get up, we are running late for church. One of the kids lost a shoe or the teenager isn't "ready." I would work myself up so much. I'd get so cranky because of the stress of not being on time, *again*, and snap at the kids.

"You are always making us late!"

They are kids. Of course their shoe is missing. It's my job as their mom to have them organize their church clothes and have them lay them out the night before, shoes and all. I've learned to make adjustments like this one, so I don't lose my temper and ruin an experience. It allows me to be in the moment more often. I want that time at Disneyland to be a happy memory of our family together, not of a mean mom forcing them to go on the Pirates of the Caribbean ride last. I want Sunday morning memories to be of peaceful family time, not a psycho mom frantically looking under beds for the missing church shoe. I've had to really work on this. Nowadays, I would honestly rather Benny go to church barefoot than lose the spirit of happiness in my home. Be busy but not rushed.

I'd be lying if I told you I have this down, but I'm progressing. Getting better and better every year. Maybe I will be perfect at it by the time they are all off to college. Just kidding. I have another affirmation for this one: "It's better to be late and loving than on time and grumpy." If this resonates with you, please adopt this as one of your new affirmations. I would rather be a little late to the school or meeting and be a nice mom than be on time and be stressed out, mean, and yelling, "Get your bags, hurry up, get in the car." The better I get at just keeping my happiness intact, I've noticed the behavior of my kids and being on time has improved.

As I'm writing this I'm laughing because just this week, I left my teenager at home when she wasn't ready to go with the rest of us. I got frustrated as we all sat out in the van waiting. "Just leave her here," I snapped at Shawn. See, I'm still working on all the things I'm teaching you.

Distractions are another reason you may have a hard time just being in the moment. So many little distractions pull our attention from our family and the things that bring us joy. Addiction is one. If you are suffering from any form of addiction, please seek professional help. Don't be prideful, assuming you can handle it yourself. The cravings of addictions rob you of your joy and so much of your life that can never be brought back.

Dependency can come in so many forms: drugs and alcohol, obviously, but also gambling, spending, and one of the hardest to overcome, pornography and sex-related addictions. Pornography is the fastest-growing habit and so incredibly addictive. You will probably be surprised to learn that one of the most common groups to become hooked on porn is eleven-year-old girls. Yep. You read that right. The Internet is so accessible. Younger and younger kids have access to anything right in the palms of their hands. Eight-year-old boys have smartphones.

I love the good that technology has done for us. During the COVID-19 pandemic, my business grew so much because we were able to pivot to online appointments with clients. I love how it can connect people. There is so much good that comes from the Internet, but we have to protect our families. We must be vigilant at this. In my home, we wait for the kids to turn thirteen before giving them a phone. They complain that "all the other kids have phones; it's not fair."

Again, I don't care what everyone else has or does. The happiness of my family is what I care about. Even at thirteen, they get a phone that doesn't have access to media at first. I don't make them be a nerd carrying around a flip phone, but there are other options out there.

Pornography is so addicting because seeing an image gives you the same addictive hit in your brain that a drug does, making you crave more. But it's even worse because, unlike drugs and alcohol that can be taken away, the image can't be taken out of your mind. You can't unsee it. When someone is looking at these things, it hurts their self-esteem, making it harder and harder to believe in themselves. When someone is suffering from addiction, it's almost impossible for them to build a Happy & Strong life. Success will continue to elude them. Their happiness is slowly eroded. The old version of them won't let the new version emerge. If you or a family member is having a hard time in this area, please get the professional help you need and put it behind you.

In the beginning phase of building a dream life and business, you will need to cut out things that are sucking up your attention and distracting you.

Let's talk now of other, more common distractions that are fighting for your true happiness. You already know how I feel about the TV and news. What are some time wasters that you have? Maybe a guilty pleasure? Everything in moderation, right? Wrong. In the beginning phase of building a dream life and business, you will need to cut out things that are sucking up your attention and distracting you. Later, once you have made it, there will be plenty of time to lay around leisurely reading your favorite magazine or mindlessly scrolling through social media.

When I was growing up, my dad would spend hours looking at car magazines. When he was employed, he would have to work long hours at his job, sometimes being gone for weeks at a time. You would think he would want to hang out with his six kids whenever he was home. Instead, he would be tinkering, fixing a car, working around the house, or doing yard work. I get it; there are always things that need to get done. But when he was inside, maybe it was too cold or too dark to work, he would sit in his chair for hours reading his car magazines. How boring.

Are carburetors really more important than me? I would ask myself. A few times I snapped my fingers in his face to get his attention. Nothing. He was totally in the zone. These days, it's cell phones. If you just look around, you see so many people completely engulfed in their phones.

A perfect example is when I was out to dinner at a restaurant recently. I walked from the hostess stand and saw a row of teenage girls sitting on a bench, all staring at their phones not talking to one another. A couple in the corner booth was staring at their phones, eating dinner without any conversation. All around this beautiful restaurant, I saw people who came to hang with one another and have a nice meal together glaring at their phones instead.

We are so caught up in our devices that it's hard to be in the moment. Over the years, I have had so many couples come to me for marriage advice. Usually, it's when they are already having problems. A huge percentage of the conversations involve social media in some way, usually Facebook.

"He is always on the phone" or "He chatted with an old girl-friend online."

Again, I love the connection and benefits that the Internet and social media can do to enhance our lives, but this is one area when way too much of a good thing can cause problems. It's not just our kids and teens who need limits on these things. Check your phone; it will tell you how many hours a day you are on social media and other apps. That's usually a lot of wasted time—time you can't get back, time that could be spent growing your relationships or your business. You can set reminders to come up after a certain amount of time passes. Maybe you start scrolling and a timer reminds you it's been fifteen minutes. It's not just social media; it's also DMs, texts, and emails that can suck your precious time away.

Shawn and I were out to a sushi dinner one night with a delightful couple. We were enjoying our delicious rolls and letting them pick our brains about building a business and parenting. About a half hour into our conversation, the wife said she had something she wanted to bring up. She was a little timid because she didn't want to throw her husband under the bus, but you could tell something was bothering her. I had been in this situation enough times to know she was about to bring up a hot spot in their marriage that they were disagreeing on. I've heard everything from "We haven't had sex in a year and a half" to "I'm not attracted to him naked." Nothing really shocks me in business mentoring sessions anymore.

People seem to feel comfortable sharing with me, and as a business mentor, I know how important the relationship between spouses is, so I am open to help wherever I can. I think they know I genuinely care about them, their marriage, and their family, so they feel safe asking me for advice in these uncomfortable situations.

Well, that night at the sushi bar wasn't one of those shockers, thank goodness. The wife simply said, "He's always on his phone."

Immediately, he started to justify why he is on the phone so much. "I need to be there when my guys have questions," he reasoned, "and I have to respond quickly." I could see in her eyes she had lost this battle several times.

"He is always checking his messages and emails. He even checks his phone when we are out to dinner on date night." She started ratting him out. "The kids and I have to fight for his attention."

I don't always take sides, but when I do, it's usually on the side of the spouse that is not in the business. This time, I just asked a simple question.

Let's put the phone down, be more productive, and be in the moment for our families.

"What time does the mail get delivered at your house?" I asked. "'My house?" He looked confused.

"Yes. What time does the mailman come?" I inquired again. "I think around three," the wife responded.

I looked at the husband and asked, "When you are at the office working and it's three o'clock, do you ever think, 'Oh my gosh, it's three. I better run home and check the mail'?"

Do you get the point I was trying to make? You wouldn't ever say, "Oh, the mailman came, I better go home as fast as I can and check the mail." Yet that's what you do every time an email, text, or DM comes in. Maybe you even have alerts for posts and other apps. Social media is designed to keep you engaged, to keep you clicking, to hopefully get you spending.

My advice to this sweet couple that night, besides trying the yummy yellowtail roll, was to check email and text messages at certain times in the day, just like you would your regular snail mail. Just because you have a message come in doesn't mean you have to respond instantly.

How about picking two or three times, at most, throughout the day to check your phone? Try to set a time when it's not as busy at work—and definitely not during family time—to respond to all your messages. What's the worst thing that could happen? You get back to people a few hours later? What's more important? I know you don't want to be that preoccupied husband, wife, mother, or father who your loved ones are asking, "Do you love me more than your phone?"

Of course, there will be times when you are waiting on a message regarding an urgent matter that will need immediate attention and response. But let's be real—those days are rare, and you can always let your loved ones know when something like that is happening. That's not what I'm talking about here. I'm speaking in general terms of your daily phone addiction. Let's put the phone down, be more productive, and be in the moment for our families. Gain some of that joy back that our devices have stolen from us.

When we wake up from the phone hypnosis, there is still the "Maybe later, honey, I am in the middle of . . . " I want to address. Again, there is always a lot to do: work to do, dinner to make, laundry that needs to be switched from the washer to the dryer— seriously endless. When one of your kids wants to play, it's easy to say, "I can't right now, maybe later." Awareness of our stress and busyness can help us be more in the moment. I realized this one day when my daughter was a toddler and asked me to play. I was in the middle of a big project, working from home. Of course, I was on the phone with someone and very irritated.

She asked if I was hungry and handed me a play plate with a plastic corn on the cob.

"I made you a snack," she said, in her sweet, nasally voice. How could I resist?

"Mmm, yummy. I am hungry. Thanks. Num num num," as I excitedly pretended to eat my delicious treat.

Her eyes lit up. "I can make you more."

As she grabbed the corn and plate and ran off to her Playschool pretend kitchen, I put my phone down and spent the next ten minutes feasting on plastic ice cream, a plastic turkey leg, and drinking from a tiny, empty cup. My daughter giggled each time she put something in her mini microwave. Finally, she said, "OK, Mom, I have to get these dishes done, but maybe later we can go feed the goats together."

I still have no idea what goats she was talking about, but the rest of the day I got my work done and I was more relaxed. *Being in the moment* and playing for just ten minutes helped lower my stress level, built a stronger relationship with my daughter, and made both of us very happy that day.

This doesn't just apply to kids; it's with your spouse too. If your spouse wants to play, then just do it. Have fun and be spontaneous. Put the phone down and play for ten minutes or maybe a little longer, hopefully. Be in the moment. I would give you some ideas here, but I think I will just leave that right there. You can come up with some fun ideas on your own, I hope.

This also goes for you. If you need a minute or two to just relax, then do it. Be in the moment. Sometimes it's hard to put things down. You have that never-ending to-do list. Take time to be in nature, meditate, or just get the needed rest or relaxation you need. We will talk soon about self-fullness, but just know that it's OK to stop and be spontaneous. Enjoy what's happening right now.

Let's talk a little more about creating memories. Many people talk about quality time versus quantity of time. Why not both? I want to schedule the time into my week, month, and year to create memories. One really easy way to do this is family traditions. I can't emphasize enough the importance of having your unique family traditions. Our family has traditions for everything. Every major holiday, we have at least one tradition. Each of the kids' birthdays has its own tradition. We even have daily traditions. In my opinion, the more the better; I can't imagine there being too many. Traditions bond families together. It's an easy way to inject more happiness into your family. Your kids will look forward to each of these traditions year after year. When they one day leave to start their own lives, it is something that will make them miss home and want to come back to visit often.

If you think about it, you probably already have some fun ones, maybe the big feast with family and friends at Thanksgiving. Another might be waking up early on Christmas morning or opening only one present on Christmas Eve. Even not opening any presents until Christmas morning can be a tradition. You see how easy this can be. First, start by writing down your current family traditions, then make a list of holidays, birthdays, and even seasons or common interests. For instance, maybe you all love *Star Wars* or a certain football team. Traditions can be built around anything.

Let me give you a few of mine to help you get started. On St. Patrick's Day, we either make corned beef in the crockpot or my kids' favorite, an all-green food meal like green eggs and ham.

For Easter, we decorate eggs. On Halloween, we carve pumpkins while listening to Halloween music, and I always roast the seeds. Decorating our tree at Christmas is a fun tradition every time. We make hot cocoa, play fun holiday music, and the whole family hangs ornaments. We reminisce over all the past Christmases as we see old decorations like "Baby's First Christmas" or the ball with a German shepherd on it from the year we got our dog.

Every year before the holiday season starts, the kids clean out old toys and books to make room for new gifts, and we bring the bags to the women's shelter. One of my favorite traditions is making hot cocoa with marshmallows and whipped cream on the first rainy day of the season and watching movies cuddled up on the couch. To be totally honest, we do this more than just that first rainy day. I love the warm summer rains when we all go outside and run and play. We will usually get our raincoats on, but there have been days that we just played tag with all our regular clothes on, finally coming in soaking wet and laughing. We used to do a popsicle party on the last day of school. I think I might bring that one back.

Do you see how traditions are a simple and inexpensive way to plan family memories? You will have a lot less of the guilty feelings from lack of family time. Some of our monthly traditions are daddy interviews with our individual children and our once-a-month fast. On the first Sunday of the month, we fast for two meals and donate the money that we would have spent on those meals. When we finally eat our dinner and break our fast, we each say what we are grateful for. A simple weekly tradition is pancakes on Sunday morning, and twice a year when we have a special church conference, we have a waffle fest! That's waffles with all the toppings. Come to think of it, maybe this one should be more often.

Two of our most important family traditions are our family councils and Sunday family day. We have a quick family meeting and assign different roles: one person conducts the meeting as we discuss any family business and upcoming events, someone gives a lesson, someone is in charge of a fun activity, and last but definitely not least, someone is in charge of the treat. You *always* have to have a treat. The kids all look forward to this time. It can be so incredibly uplifting and bonding. Other times, it's utter chaos. I usually look around and think, "*All of these people have ADHD. Why can't they just sit in their seat for a few minutes?*" Oh well, I pick my battles, and I'd rather this time as a family be a fun and enjoyable time together than me forcing them to sit still.

Some daily traditions are saying "I love you" when we hang up the phone with each other and doing family prayers. Find some traditions that work for you. My favorites are the birthday traditions. It makes the individual feel so special. Maybe the birthday boy or girl gets to pick all their favorite meals for breakfast, lunch, or dinner. We have had build-your-own pizzas several times on birthdays.

Brody's birthday tradition is that everyone in the family makes a birthday wish for him and says what they admire about him, then pops a balloon. For Daisy, we always do some sort of scavenger hunt. It's been a little harder now that she's a teenager. I've had to get way more creative than when she was little. We have done selfie scavenger hunts with all her girlfriends and treasure hunts with clues to find her hidden birthday presents. She's always loved treasure hunts and trying to figure out the next clue. Little Benny has his own special birthday plate that we use every year, and he gets to pick special treats for his birthday meals.

My favorite birthday tradition is for Austin. Every year we decorate his door. After he goes to bed the night before, I decorate his door with balloons, streamers, or pictures that his siblings drew for him. Sometimes there is a theme depending on what he is into. Even if we are out of town, I secretly pack the birthday door decorations. We have decorated RV doors when we went camping for his birthday. It's so much fun. Just try to think of a tradition unique to each family member.

I had a friend who was a busy working mom. She had so much anxiety over her kids' birthdays. She would wait until the last minute to plan the birthday and then would stress over making it so special. She would go all out and have these big elaborate parties and buy multiple presents. All of this because of the mommy guilt she was feeling. Instead of following her example, decide now on some real memory-making traditions, and when the birthdays come, just bring it up in family council meetings or your one-on-one time with that child.

"What do *you* want this year for your birthday?" You would be surprised by some of the answers.

"I just want a cake and to have my family go swimming together," was one I got from Benny.

"I want you and Dad all to myself for a day," Daisy said one year. Shawn and I took her to Harry Potter World without her brothers. Focus on creating memories. We went to Ollivanders Wand Shop, and the magic wand picked Daisy. We walked around casting spells all day. One of the witches gave her a secret spell that she could use to cut all the lines, so we went on all the rides over and over again. Finally, I felt so sick after our third time in a row on The Forbidden Journey that Shawn and I just waited as she went a few more times by herself. It truly felt like a magical day that none of us will ever forget.

> *As busy and focused as we are, fighting for our dreams, we can still be in the moment and enjoy our journey on the way there.*

Most of you know that I am pretty frugal. I don't like spending money frivolously. I ask for—and usually get—a discount on just about everything I buy. I only have a Rolex because my company gave it to me. I don't spend a ton on clothes or shopping either. The one thing I *will* spend money on is family memories. Experiences can be relived for years in our memories. We travel as a family, and that's where I splurge. Horseback riding in Montana or swimming with the dolphins in Hawaii—it's all worth it. I don't miss any chance to create a fun family memory.

One time, we went to a matinee movie, and we were the only ones in the theater. This, of course, was not planned, but I wasn't going to let an opportunity like this go by without making it special. We sat right in the middle with all kinds of snacks, popcorn, and our feet up. When the movie was done and the music for the credits

CREATING MEMORIES VERSUS GETTING THINGS DONE

was playing some hyped-up fun song, Shawn and I went down in front of the screen and started dancing. The kids looked at us for a minute, then Austin joined in. Soon we were all jumping around and dancing, having the best time. None of us remember the movie we watched that day, but we all remember the "after-party."

When we were finally walking out, I said to the kids, "Do you know how much I had to pay to have the movie theater all to ourselves so we could have this perfect day together?" They all laughed at me. "Yeah right, Mom."

As busy and focused as we are, fighting for our dreams, we can still be in the moment and enjoy our journey on the way there. Focus on creating memories, not just on getting things done.

In the next chapter, we will talk about making sure you don't screw it up once you have built it all. It can make you or break you, so I have to include it in this book for your long-term wealth and well-being. Get ready to take some serious notes on the next tip.

But first, complete the following action step for this chapter.

ACTION STEP

What are some of your best family memories? What are some traditions you want to start? Write down some ways you can create lasting memories with your family and set dates to do them.

_____

_____

_____

_____

_____

_____

_____

_____

_____

_____

12

I Can Sleep at Night

*It takes many good deeds to build a good reputation,
and only one bad one to lose it.*

Benjamin Franklin

Imagine being on vacation in paradise, maybe on a beach in Fiji, enjoying the fruit of all your years of hard work. You are debt free and have total control of your life and time. (I promise you, my friend, as good as you *think* it is to be financially independent, *it's a thousand times better*.)

You have finally made it. You are happy, tan, and relaxed. Just then, your phone rings, and it's your lawyer with bad news. Everything you worked so hard for is under attack and eventually taken away. That doesn't sound fun at all, does it?

So before we move on to how to juggle it all and scheduling tips, I have to include the importance of building a life and business on a strong foundation of integrity. I know you are making sacrifices to achieve your dreams and goals. You are spending time away from your family, probably working long hours and weekends. You believe in your vision, and obviously the price you are paying must be worth it or you wouldn't do it. It would be a shame if you put all you have into building this ideal life for yourself and have something come back later to bite you.

Make a decision to always do what's right legally and morally! There is an old proverb that says, "The first step toward greatness is to be honest." When I started in business, I saw how everyone else worked on their product knowledge and sales skills. Of course, I worked on these things too, but even more, I worked on myself. I wanted to become the type of person others would believe in, trust, and follow. Another affirmation proclaims, "We will do whatever it takes to win and never compromise our values or integrity." I sleep well at night knowing I've done what's right for my clients and teammates as well.

> *Make a decision to always do what's right legally and morally!*

This is an important step; don't blow past this one thinking, "Oh, I'm good here. I'm a good person."

I've built my business over two decades, and I have a great reputation. Because of this, I keep my clients and get referrals. My business will continue to grow, no matter what, because of the referral system I have in place. Building a dream life means you don't have the stress of looking over your shoulder in case someone complains, puts a bad review online, or even worse, forces you through the hassle and wasted time and money of a lawsuit. Having integrity doesn't just mean that you don't lie. The bottom line is whether you can be trusted along with your company and everyone in it. It also means that you don't overpromote and exaggerate. Your company's product should be so good that it practically sells itself in the right target market. I've seen so many guys overpromote their opportunities or products to get people excited. This always ends in them having to go back and explain, put out fires, and do damage control to save their reputation. Take a straightforward, honest approach and make sure everyone on your team does the same.

Sometimes one of your excited salespeople may post crazy snippets of what you do on social media. These short clips may not be enough time to fully explain, or they are taken out of context. Regulate every aspect of your business. You may not be good at paperwork, rules, and compliance, but if it's part of your company, you have to know how to do it. Master it, then delegate it. If you hand off anything to someone else—sales, compliance, training, or supervision—you must know it first, so you can hold your delegates accountable. *If your client or teammate can't trust you in* one thing, *they won't trust you in* anything.

The same goes for anyone in your company. If the client doesn't feel they can trust one person or one part of your system, they won't trust you or your company's products in general. You may not think this is a big deal. Let me explain. I know that every person out there knows tons of people. They probably have hundreds of contacts in their cell phone alone. If they have an outstanding experience with me or my company, they will more than likely tell others. Even more so, they will for sure spread the word if they have a *bad* experience.

As I mentioned, I have a Code of Honor in my company that all my teammates agree to. Our number-one policy is "Mission first. Team second. Self last." Mission means always do what's right for the client. Team second means having a team player mentality. ("Team over me" is another affirmation of mine.) Self is referring to your profit. If you take good care of others, money will come.

Here's another policy from our Code of Honor: "Treat all appointments like gold and do your best with every one of them."

That means not canceling on a little client to schedule a big one. It means treating the smallest client the same as your whale. I have had clients for whom all I did was sit with them and educate them on how to get out of debt. I didn't make a dime, but they loved me, they enjoyed the whole process they experienced with my company, and they ended up referring me to all their friends and their rich uncle.

Make sure you can always answer yes to this question: "Have you been fair and honest in *all* your dealings with your fellow man?" This applies now to all areas of your life, not only in business. If you can answer yes, then you can always sleep well at night and not have anything come back later to take it all away from you.

Have you been fair and honest in all your dealings with your fellow man?

This includes being honest on taxes and even when you underpaid for something by mistake. You definitely don't want crazy, long, drawn-out tax audits distracting you from your family or your business. Nothing about that is Happy & Strong. Keep good records and find a super-aggressive CPA who will work hard to find you every possible write-off. Find someone who will save you money but is honest and stays in the lines, then sleep well knowing you are OK in this area too.

I believe in the law of the harvest. You reap what you sow. If you are dishonest, it comes back around. There is always the harvest. You can't get away with being unethical—not in the long run. You may for a little while, but eventually there will be the harvest. Some call it karma. Why work so hard for so long building your dream life if you are still stressed about what *could* happen? I'm not interested in cutting corners to make it happen faster. The only shortcut is to do it right the first time. It works the other way around as well. I know if I treat others right, am honest, and always try to help and add value to the lives of others, I will eventually harvest the same. It's a way of building in my own luck.

I said it before and I will say it again: watch who you associate with. Your associations define you. The number one thing I look for when hiring someone is strength of character. I can train them on just about everything in business, but it's hard to instruct them when they are dishonest. It's not worth my time to try. If you have people in your company with serious character issues, you have to get rid of them. This may sound judgmental to you. No one is perfect, so I'm not talking about minor things. I can work through most issues and hopefully help others grow if possible. I'm all for second chances. I've given people the benefit of the doubt and multiple chances when they make mistakes, but when they have serious character issues, I have to let them go. I'm talking about when someone intentionally steals, cheats, or lies. You have to protect your family and business for the long term.

Years ago, I had a talented young man who worked on my sales team. He was incredible with clients. He was great at our business, but he kept sleeping with all the girls, some of whom were married women. He also was married. At first, I couldn't believe it.

"They must have just misread something. He's such a good guy," I thought. He was very friendly and had that smoldering smile that charmed everyone. This might have been one of the reasons he was so good with clients. He was also my top guy.

Sometimes I have seen people in business look the other way on minor character issues because the problem guy happens to be the "cash cow." They don't want to offend and lose him, so they let him get away with minor ethical violations, as long as no laws are broken. In today's world, any sexual harassment complaints must be taken seriously, but in this case, there were no complaints. The girls were infatuated with him and hooked up with him without protest. It was everyone else on the team who didn't like hearing about it.

In his mind, his sex life had nothing to do with business; therefore, it was none of my business. Now, even though no laws or rules were broken, I couldn't keep letting this happen. Marriages were being affected, and our reputation as a company of integrity was at stake. I wanted all the women, and of course all the spouses of the women on my team, to feel safe and comfortable.

It really hurt to let him go. I cared about him and his family. I felt sad for his wife and daughter. For a while, I second-guessed my decision to stop working with him. Was I being too harsh? Too overly critical? Once he was gone, so many women came forward to share similar stories about him. They finally felt safe to tell me what had happened to them. I'm glad my decision here wasn't thinking short term about how much money I would lose. It was one of those "team over me" decisions. By doing what is right for the long-term well-being of the whole team, it always turns out to be what is also best for you. If someone is a liar or unethical, it's best to get them off the team. It will eventually become a cancer that hurts your reputation or, worse, hurts people. Even if it costs you financially now, it is what's best for you and everyone in your company in the long term.

This is why it's so important to guard your associations. Make sure the people you follow in business and any mentors you decide to take coaching from also have the same value system as you. If they don't, it will cause you undue stress. They may do something or encourage you to do something that will hurt you, your family, your business, or your reputation.

Also don't forget, your kids are always watching your example. William Shakespeare said, "No legacy is so rich as honesty." Remember fair and honest in all your dealings? If you go through the line at Disneyland and tell your thirteen-year-old, "You're twelve if anyone asks," what kind of message are you sending? Is it OK to lie "sometimes"? Integrity is doing what's right and true, no matter what. No matter if anyone is around and no one will ever know. You are going to hate this next story, but I will tell you anyway.

I was leaving a local craft store called Michaels and started to load my bags into the back of my car. I noticed a ribbon in the bottom of the cart that I forgot to pay for and went back inside. No one would have ever known, and I'm sure Michaels wouldn't have been hurting too much over the ninety-nine cents that the ribbon cost. But *I* knew, and I don't want anything but good coming back to me at harvest time. I stood there with my ribbon and receipt as the cashier looked at me annoyed. If you were in line that day you probably would have given me dirty looks like everyone else did as I held up the line to fix my mistake. It was uncomfortable, but I left feeling good.

Make sure the people you follow in business and any mentors you decide to take coaching from also have the same value system as you.

I sleep well every night knowing I've been fair, honest, and treated people right. I also know I have had it come back to me countless times. What goes around comes around, and I have been blessed beyond measure with amazing people and opportunities that helped me along the way.

I know integrity isn't the most fun topic, and I'm sure you are a very honest and good person. But always remember how important core values and morality are when building a Happy & Strong future.

The next chapter is on self-fullness, which is one of my favorite subjects in life. Wellness and self-care are things I neglected for a long time, and trust me, my body paid the price for it. I'm excited to share with you what I've learned (mostly from my mistakes). But before you move on, take a moment to complete the following action step.

ACTION STEP

Write down some of the times in your life where you know you did the right thing and how that made you feel. How does it make you feel now, remembering those moments?

_____

_____

_____

_____

_____

_____

_____

_____

_____

_____

13

PUT ON YOUR OWN OXYGEN MASK FIRST

Self-care is giving the best of you, instead of what's left of you.

KATIE REED

Most people usually worry about their health only when something is wrong with their body. You learn to eat healthy because your doctor orders you to. The same goes for your mental health. You learn to take care of it because you are not so happy and not so strong. If you are a super-driven maniac like me I'm sure you are totally inspired by your vision. I used to say: I eat, sleep, and breathe [whatever my goal was].

Every day I was doing all I could to move closer to making my dream a reality. My family was counting on me to make it happen.

By 9 a.m., I was on appointments, and then I worked as late as I could. I sometimes forgot to eat; I was so focused. Of course, having kids changed that somewhat. I had to make adjustments and plan in all the family things. I never forgot to feed my kids. I continued to work hard on my business as well as raising little ones. I did Mommy and Me classes, cooked dinner, attended church service, helped with all the challenges people in my business were going through, and tried to be a supportive, loving wife. I just kept adding things to my already overflowing plate.

This is how I saw the world and the order that I would respond:

First, things that needed to get done. The urgent needs of everyone around me. I had to call back clients, put together a lesson for church, get groceries, do that mentoring call, and so on.

Second, the kids. Making sure all their needs were being met, school was going well, and they were happy.

Third, my husband. After all I had to do, poor Shawn wasn't getting the attention he deserved, but at least he is an adult, right? He could feed himself if he had to. Wrong! Your marriage won't take care of itself.

Last of all, myself. I never thought of myself as a priority. "I will sleep later," I would reason. "No big deal if I eat fast food," I thought. I told myself, "I'm young and healthy, and now is the time to make it happen." I never really thought of my health as a priority. I didn't do drugs, drink alcohol, or even drink coffee. I thought of myself as a pretty healthy person. Most people have this same rationale.

I've made some incredible lifestyle changes. Now, I make sure *my* needs are being met first. I have to take care of *me*. If I'm tired, sick, or stressed out, I am no good to anyone. There is no way I can be the best version of myself. I won't be the best mom or business leader, and I won't giving it my all in the church and other responsibilities I have. So now after I make sure I am good on self-care, my husband and marriage come second, my children and family are next, and last is all the other urgent things pulling at me day to day.

When I first started making my self-care a priority, I felt a little guilty. I would think that maybe I should be helping one of the kids with something, working or planning something; I shouldn't just be wasting time.

I want you to really pay attention to this chapter. Would you be happy if you made millions of dollars, only to turn around and have to spend it all on doctors trying to buy back the health you sacrificed? I've seen so many people neglect their health on their way to the top. They have heart attacks and high blood pressure, and all kinds of serious health problems plague them and steal their dream. This is *not* Happy & Strong.

> *Would you be happy if you made millions of dollars, only to turn around and have to spend it all on doctors trying to buy back the health you sacrificed?*

There is so much I could teach you about this subject. I could write a whole other book on physical and mental wellness. How do you think I learned so much about it? You probably guessed it—I got a crash course when I neglected it for too long and made myself sick.

One Sunday morning while getting ready for church, Shawn noticed I was losing my hair.

"You have a little bald spot or something," he said, pointing to the back of my head.

He was being kind.

I looked in the mirror and holy crap, I saw a *giant* bald spot. It was an oval about three inches long and two inches wide. It was bald as could be, no hair at all. I had noticed a few days before that more hair was coming out in my hairbrush and in the shower. I freaked out, tied my hair into a ponytail, and booked an appointment with the doctor right away. The next day, I sat worrying on the table in my doctor's office.

"Could it be stress related?" I asked, hoping for something simple and treatable, and not that I'm dying or something.

He casually went through his series of questions and finally asked to see the back of my head. When I took out my ponytail, his eyes just about popped out.

"Oh no, this is more than stress, this is autoimmune," he said. "You need to go see a rheumatologist right away. You are sick. I will give you a few names and see who is in your network of doctors, but schedule it immediately."

That is how my wellness journey began.

Next, I went to the rheumatologist as suggested. Not fun. I gave what seemed like fifty vials of blood then sat again waiting for answers. A female doctor around my age came in. She seemed confident and condescending. She rattled off a list of symptoms and asked if I were experiencing any of them.

"Yes. Yep. Yes." I was experiencing most of them from time to time. Every time I had random aches and pains, dry eyes and mouth, and other ailments, I had just shrugged it off and thought it was from being tired. I was an exhausted mom of three and always on the go. It wasn't until my hair fell out that I even paid attention. The doctor went on to say she thought I had lupus. OK, good. Finally, I could get some answers.

"What's lupus? What causes it? How do you cure it?" I asked eagerly.

"No cure, and we don't know what causes it. It could be your lipstick for all we know," she said quickly in a very matter-of-fact tone. Then she went on to prescribe some medication.

"We will start you off on this and see how it goes, but more than likely we will have to go to something stronger. By the way, I'm also going to give you a prescription for a base eye exam because this pill will eventually ruin your eyesight. And from now on, you can't get pregnant ever again because this medication is harmful to a fetus."

What? I was confused. *She "thinks" I have lupus and there is no cure but is giving me this horrible medication!*

"Shouldn't we wait until we know more before I start taking meds?" I asked.

She quickly snapped, "What do you want to wait for? Your kidneys to fail?"

I took the papers from her hand and read that I had undifferentiated connective tissue disorder. Basically, I had an autoimmune disease attacking my connective tissue. It made sense, all the pains in the ligaments around my joints and other weird symptoms I had been having for months. She said she knew it was lupus but just couldn't rule out a few other autoimmune diseases such as Crohn's disease and rheumatoid arthritis.

I thought of all the training I had gone through about staying positive and not listening to negative people. I left that doctor's office and decided to never see her again. I didn't take her pills either. Instead, I decided to set a goal. This time instead of a business goal, I set a goal to be in perfect health. I never listened to negative people before, and I wasn't going to start now. I'm not saying that all doctors are negative—if you are sick, definitely go see an expert. But this doctor wasn't for me.

I became a student of my body. I learned everything there was about my so-called "incurable" disease. I learned about alternative methods of healing my body. I changed my diet, my exercise, and movement. I got out in nature more, and I became the expert of my personal wellness. I hated reading all those books about your gut health and good versus bad bacteria. I searched out experts and asked girlfriends of mine who knew how to eat a clean diet to come over and teach me.

One day, my good friend Heather came over. She taught me how to read labels properly and identify bad ingredients. She cleaned out my pantry, and there were literally maybe three things left on the shelves.

"Gross!" she would say as she tossed something in the trash. "Rancid!" With a look of disgust, out went my cooking oils.

"This isn't even food. This really should not go in the human body." Wow. I didn't realize how bad my diet was.

I set a date for eighteen months to be more than autoimmune free. I was going to be healthy, happy, and strong. Like any other goal, I wrote it down and read it daily. I stuck to my new horribly restrictive diet, never cheating. When I would feel my lupus pains, I would become so discouraged. *Was it working at all?* I wondered.

I was going to be healthy, happy, and strong. Like any other goal, I wrote it down and read it daily.

My new rheumatologist was way more positive and open to natural healing.

"When you clean house, Jaime, you stir up dust. It might get worse before it gets better," my doctor would say when I felt discouraged.

I wanted to quit a thousand times. It was so hard. It really did get worse before it got better. I lost so much weight, about thirty pounds. My hips, collar bones, and ribs were sticking out, my eyes looked sunken in, and I had no energy. Walking up my stairs to the second floor became too much. My muscles would fatigue, and I would have to stop halfway up to rest. My hair was so thin, and just about everything I ate gave me a bad reaction.

One afternoon, I was lying on my couch. I had no strength in my body. Lying there motionless, I could hear Daisy and Austin playing upstairs. They started to argue over some toy. My emotions got the best of me as I stayed right there feeling horrible. I couldn't even move; I knew I wouldn't make it up those stairs. I felt the hot tears rolling down my face and soaking the couch cushion.

I'm the worst mom. I can't even take care of my kids, I thought as I heard the two of them getting louder.

I just laid there crying, feeling sad and weak, wondering if I was depressed and if I would ever be myself again. More than anything, I wanted to be happy again. I stuck to the diet and new routine and slowly improved my health. Every three months, I had to do lab work. "Whatever you are doing, keep it up," my doctor would say cheerfully. "You can tell me you are feeling better, but the labs don't lie. It's definitely working."

I kept learning and applying everything I was taught. I figured out food can be medicine. I had a wonderful natural medicine doctor named Brian Carrico as well as my Eastern medicine doctors, Dr. Na and Dr. Yoon. They helped me figure out a specific diet that works for me. I kept reading all my goals, including my health and wellness goals, every day. I started to visualize the day my doctor would look at my labs and say I was no longer sick. It was the same month that I had written in my plan. I went to go get my labs done. I sat anxiously as he pulled out the huge file on me and started going through the normal routine and reading off all my markers and numbers. When he was done, he looked at me and leaned in a little. He took out his pen and drew a line on the thin paper that covers the patient table.

"You are finally on this side of the fence, Jaime," he said as he pointed to his drawing. "Don't stop doing what you are doing. Get as far away from the fence as possible." He smiled. "Good job, girl, you are no longer autoimmune; you completely reversed it."

That was several years ago. My health since then has been a huge priority. The way I eat, sleep habits, stress levels, and mental health are all so important now. It's kind of like when I started having kids and had to make tweaks and adjustments; that's exactly what I did. My goals and dreams didn't change. I kept going after them; I just made sure I took care of myself first. I will give you my opinion here on health and wellness, but I'm not a doctor or a dietitian. Everyone's body and needs are different. All I can share is what my journey so far has taught me and what has made a difference in my life as a busy entrepreneur.

The basics of wellness are get enough rest, eat right, and exercise. If you neglect any one of these three majors for too long, your body will start to fight back.

Let's start with sleep. I used to be such a night owl. I was always working late into the evening, thinking that after the kids go to bed, I can get so much work done. When you're younger, you can get away with this to some degree, but it will catch up to you eventually. The basics of wellness are get enough rest, eat right, and exercise. If you neglect any one of these three majors for too long, your body will start to fight back.

I need a good eight hours now. Sleep is where your body builds and restores itself. If you are staying up too late or waking up restlessly during the night, this is going to take its toll on your mental and physical wellbeing. When you are not getting enough good sleep, you seem to age faster and heal slower. It will literally make you sick. Some interesting studies on sleep have shown that it can affect how positive we are. Sleep-deprived people had a harder time remembering pleasant memories. They were able to recall more gloomy memories and were more sensitive to negative emotions. Let me give you a few tips on how to improve your sleeping habits.

1. *First, make sure to be more consistent with your bedtime and wake times.* This will aid in the quality of sleep you are getting. Your body has a natural time clock. Getting outside and being in the sun during the day will also help your body keep a natural rhythm and relax better when it's time to go to bed. If you are cooped up in your home or office all day and not getting any sunlight, it will throw off your body's natural rhythm and can cause insomnia.

2. *Obviously, limit the amount of caffeine at night.* For me, it's chocolate. Caffeine can affect sleep patterns even if taken six to eight hours before bed.

3. *In general, don't drink too much of anything before bed.* Drinking too many liquids right before bed may result in you waking up to use the bathroom. I know when I wake up to go to the bathroom at night, I can't fall back asleep. Alcohol at night can also affect your sleep hormones and cause disruptions.

4. *Make your bedroom conducive for a good night's sleep, eliminating noise and light that can keep you awake.* Maybe there is an annoying light from an alarm clock or DVD player that needs to be removed.

5. *Find the temperature that works for you.* Make sure your bedroom is a place that is comfortable and enjoyable to you, not too hot or too cold. Temperature can affect you even more than noise sometimes. Get a comfy mattress and pillows.

6. *Stay off your phone or tablet before bed.* The blue light that they give off reduces the production of the hormone melatonin, which helps you relax and get deep sleep.

There are now blue-light blocking glasses and apps you can download that may help. Honestly, though, the best thing to do is turn off the TV and screens two hours before you want to fall asleep. Instead of scrolling social media, get some extra cuddle time in or read a good book. You will get a more restful sleep, wake up with more energy, and have a healthier body.

If you still are having a problem relaxing and turning off your brain, a melatonin supplement may help. It's safe and not addicting in any way. I have lavender essential oil in my nightstand that I will put in a diffuser or on my pillow.

How about exercise? Exercise contributes to your health as well as your overall happiness and well-being. Some people love exercise and fitness; it's just part of who they are. Others hate it, and it seems impossible to stick to a routine. I don't have to tell you how important exercise is for your body—any doctor in the world will tell you that. If you want to lose weight or have a more energetic, healthy, fit body, you need to exercise. But it's so much more than that. Just like with sleep, if I don't get my exercise in, I am more cranky and less productive. Regular exercise helps increase brain power. It also helps improve your own body image, which boosts your self-esteem.

When I stick to a good routine, I'm so much happier and more fun to be around. Exercise is not just for my body, it's for my mental health. I'm a more patient mother and business leader. I'm clearer in my thoughts, and I actually sleep better. Just don't exercise right before bed. This may keep you from being able to relax and fall asleep quickly.

When I worked at the gym, I exercised daily. I lifted weights pretty much every day. I had a strong, fit body but probably overdid it on the squats and heavy lifting. My knees and lower back pay for it today.

Once I really got focused in business, I stopped working out for a long time. I would stop by a drive-thru for lunch as I rushed around between appointments. My body became sluggish; I gained some weight, and I had a lot of brain fog. I would sit for long periods of time at my desk, and my back started to really bother me. A bulging disk had developed, and I found myself having to go to physical therapy in my thirties.

I made about every mistake there is with wellness. Hopefully I can help others skip over the same mistakes I made. Once I had made the decision to be Happy & Strong, there were no more excuses. I had to keep my body healthy and fit.

If you are not working out yet, just start. Pick something you enjoy. It doesn't have to be in a gym or anything that is intimidating. You may want to have a trainer help you establish a routine. Try different workouts until you find something you like. If you are into a certain sport, join a league. Try to make it fun so you are more likely to stick to it. If you have never worked out and feel overwhelmed with where to begin, start with walking. Get your body moving. Set a timer on your phone for twenty minutes and walk around outside. When your timer goes off, turn around and walk back home.

Once I had made the decision to be Happy & Strong, there were no more excuses. I had to keep my body healthy and fit.

If possible, I like to do my workouts outdoors. Being in nature is so much more healing to me. I love Pilates, but I will walk, hike, and sometimes do fun martial arts workouts to get my cardio in. You can go online and find tons of free YouTube videos for stretching, yoga, and every other fitness program you can think of. Most of my workouts nowadays are functional strength training with a focus on core. I also recommend you get a foam roller and learn how to use it properly; trust me, it's a total game-changer.

I see a lot of my business competition plateau or burn out. I don't burn out because I treat my body right. I understand how to get optimal long-term performance out of my body while also maintaining happiness and mental wellness. The start and stop of burnout is something that I'm not interested in. I also don't want to ever go through the sickness I went through in the past. These are the things that I learned and applied that have helped me, and I hope they will help you too. Everyone wants to be in shape and healthy, but they don't know where to start and they lack the discipline to stay on track.

Now let's talk about food. (Remember, I'm only the messenger.) I often get asked about my diet.

"Jaime, what's your diet? I heard you eat really well" or "I heard you cured yourself from lupus, what diet do you follow?"

I hate talking about my diet. My diet might be very different than what is right for you. Our bodies are all unique. I have spent a lot of time figuring out my health code. I know what food is *my* medicine. I suggest you become a student of your body. I will give you some basics, though, to get you started.

Plan ahead. This will help a lot. If you have a busy day at the office, pack a lunch so that you are not tempted to run to a drive-thru. If you are traveling, you can figure out ahead of time where to stop to eat.

Avoid fast food. If you absolutely have to eat on the go and your only option is a quick restaurant, try to find healthier alternatives like Sharkey's or Chipotle. They have organic options.

Meal plan and make big batches of food on the weekend to freeze. This will also help you save time during the hectic weekdays. This way you have several healthy meals. When you get home from the grocery store, prep your food so that you have convenient, healthy snacks.

Avoid processed food. Processed means anything that comes out of a box or a can. Eat real, whole food instead. Try to eat fruits and vegetables and foods that haven't been changed, processed, preserved, or packed. No soda. Just removing soda will make a huge difference.

Eat organic if possible. Go online and google "the dirty dozen." This will list the foods that you should only eat organic. For example, berries. Berries grow on the ground. They are sprayed with pesticides and herbicides and then covered with a protection that makes the sprays stick so they aren't washed away in the rain. The soil the berries grow in has all these same poisons in it. Would you eat a strawberry that was sprayed with poisonous ant spray? Of course not. Would you let your child eat one, even if you washed it off? I wouldn't. There are certain fruits and vegetables that are OK to not eat organic and some that are just too harmful to your system.

Our Western diet is full of processed foods, pesticides, antibiotics, and other harmful things that are just too hard on our system. Over time, this will do a lot of damage to your digestive tract. Look what happened to me. My body developed an autoimmune disease. This is so common among adults right now. Autoimmunity means the body is attacking itself; in my case, it was attacking the connective tissue. I don't believe the body would attack itself for no reason; the human body is designed to heal itself. Think of when you get a scratch and break open the skin; you might put a Band-Aid on it, and a few days later, there is a scab and then a scar. It healed. The human body is amazing.

We put such crappy things into our body. We are exposed to so many pollutants that our body gets confused and attacks cells to get rid of these things. I did a detox and went to a completely clean diet for eighteen months. No processed food, no gluten, no processed sugar, no soy, no dairy, and a few other things. It was the worst. Gluten and sugar wreak havoc on your system. Not everyone is allergic to gluten, but it's not good for anyone. For me, it's my kryptonite. Even though I am autoimmune-free and have been for years, I have added all but gluten back into my diet. It makes me sick every time I accidentally eat it. A low sugar, whole food, and gluten-free diet is the best start if you are unhealthy and trying to figure out what is wrong with your body.

Keep a food log and track what you eat. Every time you get sick, look for patterns. Maybe you have chronic fatigue, aches and pains, brain fog, or digestive problems. When symptoms arise, go back and see what you ate that could be causing the issues. Become a student of your body. Keeping a food log also helped me to watch what I was eating and notice unhealthy patterns of skipping meals or late-night snacking.

Seek out mentors in health and fitness. You do this for business, so why not for your wellness? You can find tons of information online and in books. I wouldn't have been able to cure my autoimmunity without the books I read, my three amazing mentors (Dr. Carrico, Dr. Na, and Dr. Yoon), and other friends who helped me along the way.

Find out if you have allergies. When I figured out that I was allergic to gluten, my health became much easier to manage. I had my natural medicine doctors create a diet that was perfect for my body. There are now companies online that offer blood tests. They will send you a kit in the mail, and then they will give you a list of all the foods you are possibly sensitive to.

Learn to read labels and understand ingredients. I can't stress to you enough the importance of learning how to read ingredients. Just because something says gluten-free or organic doesn't mean it's good for you. My mom was so excited one day because she bought some "healthy" juice at Walmart. It was a big gallon-size juice for ninety-nine cents. That should have been a clue that it wasn't healthy. She was asking if I thought the kids would like it.

"It's sugar-free," she said, pointing to the name on the jug that had the word "natural" in the title. I looked at the back and simply read the ingredients to her. Everything you buy in the store must have a list of what's in it. I couldn't pronounce most of the ingredients, then there were yellow and red dyes and some mango-flavored concentrate.

"The reason it's sugar-free is because it's not real juice. Real fruit has some sugar," I explained to her.

Read labels. Generally speaking, the fewer ingredients, the better, and make sure you can pronounce them.

Stay away from diet fads. Instead, listen to your body. Diet fads come and go. I remember when agave was all hyped up as a healthy sugar alternative, and everyone thought it was super healthy. Keto, paleo, all of these can be good, but first you have to figure out if they are good for *you* and your specific body. I've seen so many people torture themselves for weeks on some diet trend just to go back to all their bad habits as soon as it was over. You have to want to be healthier, which is more of a lifestyle change. Just eating cleaner can be a good start.

You have to want to be healthier, which is more of a lifestyle change.

Remember to stay hydrated. The bene-fits of drinking water are too many to list here. Just know that it helps keep every system in your body functioning properly. I start my day with a full glass of water, even before I get out of bed. This is important to start my digestive tract the right way. Think about it: you have been sleeping all night. The body has been fasting and needs hydration.

Think of the grass in the heat of August. It turns yellow and dies. That is what your body is like without enough water. You won't function optimally, and you won't have the energy levels to do all that you want to do.

There are different recommendations about how much water to drink in a day. One of the biggest factors is how much you weigh. Men should generally drink more than women.

It also depends on where you live. If you live in hot, dry climates you will need more. In the warmer summer seasons, in higher altitudes, or if you are very active, you may need more water due to perspiration.

You also have to factor in your diet and how healthy you are. If you drink a lot of coffee or eat a very salty or sugary diet, you need more water. And, of course, if you are sick, pregnant, or breast-feeding, you need extra water to stay hydrated.

Next, lower your toxic load. Wash all fruits and vegetables (again, buy organic when possible). Use fewer chemicals in your household cleaning products. Try not to use toxins inside or around your house. If at all possible, go green when it comes to pesticides and sprays for your garden. Even your lotions and the things you put on your skin can be more natural. Glass food storage containers are better for you than plastic. Drink filtered water. All these toxins add up.

Self-care is important. You have to set boundaries for yourself so that you don't get overextended and stress yourself out. Give yourself permission to say no when needed. Too much pressure and tension and you will not only be run down but you will also start to be resentful. Stress can be just as harmful to your body as eating badly. It releases damaging toxins into your system. Find ways to reduce or manage your stress and anxiety daily.

Again, regular exercise will help. You can also try listening to music, spending more time with friends, helping others, or meditation. Look online for ideas on controlled breathing techniques. Meditation clears the mind and helps you feel calmer. It is proven to help you have a happier life because it fosters a feeling of contentment. It also helps you develop more empathy and awareness.

I have a hard time relaxing. Meditation was something I never thought I would get good at.

When I was having my first baby, we went to Lamaze class; it was a nightmare. Have you ever had to go to Lamaze? It's the worst. I was big and pregnant and tired. I had to bring Shawn because he was supposed to be my partner in all this. We started the class, and the instructor immediately got on my nerves. She was the super crunchy granola type and kept saying weird stuff like, "Listen to your inner aura."

In my final weeks of pregnancy, I was just not in the mood for that. We were all on mats on the floor, practicing breathing. The lights were dimmed, and the breathing was supposed to help us relax. But it made me more anxious. Halfway through, I looked behind me and Shawn was asleep. Of course he was. So typical. This is a guy who has fallen asleep in the middle of a parent-teacher conference on more than one occasion. Not joking. The teacher and I will look over and he will be sitting up in one of those little miniature chairs, eyes closed and sleeping.

"Really?!" I jabbed my elbow into his side. I was so mad. Lamaze didn't work. I couldn't do it. It is supposed to help you feel more confident in the child birthing process. Yeah, right. We left the class, and I felt like a failure. "I don't even want to push this baby out!" I whined. "This is going to be horrible. Why can't I relax?"

Since then, a few mentors have suggested meditation or breathing exercises to reduce stress. It actually does help. If you have a hard time getting into it or turning off the million thoughts going on in your head, maybe download a meditation app to help get you started. If at first it doesn't work, don't give up. When I first began meditation, I would sit there thinking about other things I had to get done, annoyed at myself for wasting time.

Prayer is another form of meditation that helps with stress.

If you feel you have too much to handle and none of these ideas seem to work, seeing a therapist might be helpful. It's OK to seek therapy; sometimes just being able to talk to someone and get it all out will really help. Therapists are trained to teach you coping skills, so even if you go for only a few sessions and you learn some great new ways to deal with stress, it would be worth the time. Most insurance companies will cover it, and it can't hurt. Don't be ashamed to seek help. If you had a toothache, you would schedule a dentist appointment. If you had stomach pains or your body was ill, you would go see a doctor. If you are not mentally well, why not see an expert? It just makes sense.

Your wellness is so important to your personal happiness. Figure out what your personal needs are. Some people really need solitude, to be left alone for a while. Others need human affection and social-izing. Some need recognition for all their hard work or to be challenged in some way. Others need physical contact, the hugs, high-fives, and play. Spend some time discovering what your needs are and what helps you unwind and feel good. Being self-full is not the same as being selfish. It's hard to pour yourself into others when you are empty.

It's hard to pour yourself into others when you are empty.

Self-care isn't just what we see on social media. Sure, it can be doing a spa day or getting your nails done, but it can also be taking time to go fishing or go on a hike. That's not what I would pick as self-care, but what matters is that you take care of *you*. If you need to take a day and just relax doing something you love, do it. Pamper yourself.

I have a compulsive need to plan and feel like I am on top of everything. I figured out that I can schedule in my calendar to happily waste time. Sounds funny, but it is totally relaxing. I schedule one day off a month to do anything but work. I journal, work out, maybe go get a smoothie or a massage. Sometimes, I will go to Michaels or some cute boutique to walk the aisles and buy little things. Other times, I will sit by the fire and rewrite my goals and dreams and try to stretch my own vision of what's possible. I may just do a long lunch with a friend. It's scheduled time that is happily wasted. I completely decompress, and I usually get the best ideas afterward for my business because I was able to relax. That's just me. Figure out what works for you. You need to sharpen the ax somehow. Otherwise, you will stress out and burn out.

Just remember that when things get crazy and it seems too hard, it's just personal growth you are going through. Take a look at your life. What adjustments and tweaks need to be made? Make them, but don't quit. If you are feeling tired or burned out, fine. Take a nap, but don't quit. Keep moving forward, even if you go a little slower for a while. Don't give up.

I mentioned it before, but I think it's important enough to say again: always be working on *you*. Part of making yourself and self-care a priority is self-improvement. This is never-ending. Read good books and listen to audiobooks and podcasts. Keep upgrading you. I always want to be getting better. I read books on business, spirituality, scriptures, parenting, marriage, uplifting true stories, autobiographies, communication, and how the brain works. There is just so much to learn, and I have so much room for improvement. I want to be better today than yesterday. Never settle! Never settle for who you are right now, but still be happy.

My friend Ed Mylett calls it "blissfully dissatisfied." No matter where you are working like a maniac to get to, you have to know how to find joy in the journey as you are going there. You want to be more, do more, and are dissatisfied with where you are now, but you can still enjoy the moment and be happy.

Hellen Keller said, "Be happy with what you have while working for what you want." Learn to keep stretching yourself to be better, but you can be happy today while you grow toward greatness and are becoming the next version of you.

My friend, please make sure your self-care is always a priority. Put yourself at the top of your to-do list. Next, I want to make sure that once you get to where you are going, you don't blow it. So in the following chapter, I will teach you one of the most important success lessons of all. But first, take a moment to complete the following action step.

ACTION STEP

*Write down any ideas or action steps you want to imple-
ment to have a healthier lifestyle.*

_____

_____

_____

_____

_____

_____

_____

_____

_____

_____

_____

_____

14

DON'T BLOW IT

*It's not how much money you make, but how much
money you keep, how hard it works for you, and how
many generations you keep it for.*

ROBERT KIYOSAKI

When I say, "Happy & Strong," that includes being financially strong.

I knew a guy who made millions of dollars. He had an incredible business and sold it for hundreds of millions. He then spent all
his time spending that money. All of it.

It was all ego-driven. He built the biggest house in his state.
It had a bowling alley, a full movie theater with a concession
stand and box office, a golf course, several guest houses, and a car
museum full of exotic and classic cars. He had glass imported from
other countries. His wife's closet was bigger than my whole house

at that time. Unfortunately, he blew through all his money in about ten years. That's more than stupid; that's insanity.

So many people work hard, achieve the income they've been chasing after, and then blow it all. Excited about finally "making it," they buy the big house and fancy cars, spending everything they make. You have to learn the basics of handling money well. Learn how money works and how it can be a tool to help you leverage and build. It can provide a great life for your family.

Being Happy & Strong means you live the life you dreamed of for your family, but it also means having peace of mind.

On the outside, so many people look like they are living the dream. They have big homes but small bank accounts. The reality is it doesn't matter how much you make if you are spending it all. Wealth is built only when you are saving.

I know it's tempting to keep up with the Joneses. It's easy to justify in your mind. This is why you have worked so hard; you deserve it. You have paid a price for success, made sacrifices, and want to have nice things. I get it, but I want to warn you against extravagance and careless spending.

Are the designer clothes and handbags that important? More important than your future dreams? Do you really need the big screen TV? Who are you really trying to impress? Your neighbor during Super Bowl? You don't need all that right now. There is a season for everything. We live during a time of wastefulness. People want immediate gratification and are easily seduced by lavish lifestyles. Just because you are making more money doesn't mean you have to upgrade your lifestyle right away. Being Happy & Strong means you live the life you dreamed of for your family, but it also means having peace of mind. *Save first.*

Unexpected ups and downs are likely to happen that are outside of your control. Your industry could change, laws or regulations may change. I went through the 9/11 tragedy, then the 2008 financial crisis. Now we've all seen and experienced firsthand a worldwide pandemic. The COVID-19 crisis put so many people out of business. I want you to work hard and taste the victory of achieving everything you've dreamed of for your family. I want you to live an *amazing* life, but I also want you to be prepared for anything that comes your way. If there is another unexpected catastrophe, you won't be impacted financially.

During each of these uncertain times, my business and my income grew. This had a lot to do with the fact that I could react without the emotion of panic driven by lack of financial security. All I did was pivot and make the necessary adjustments. I had plenty of money saved so that even if my income temporarily stopped, I was fine, and all my bills were easily paid. I never had to dip into savings or get a loan. In times of chaos, it is usually a great time for growth and evolving as a company. In the Chinese language, the symbol for the word "crisis" is the same as it is for the word "opportunity." After 2008, so many people lost their homes. The stock market took a hit and the housing market fell. While some were having the worst of times, others who had cash were buying up properties at a deep discount. Some business owners went into panic management and started making bad decisions because of their low cash reserves. For me, I just focused on relationships and helping others. Never once did I make a decision based on money; it was always what was best long term for my clients and for my company.

Even though I have been in the financial industry for over twenty years, I won't give you any specific financial advice. Every family and individual has different goals and needs. Start becoming more financially literate. Search out good financial professionals whom you trust. I can only speak here in very basic terms, as a friend, on what I have seen work in my life. Before I give you a few tips on building wealth, my biggest advice I can give you is *save!* Live within your means! Cash is king! Yes, plan for the long term and learn about all the great places to invest, but also have a high amount of cash reserves. Stop spending and start saving.

I love this great quote from Will Rogers: "The quickest way to double your money is to fold it in half and put it in your back pocket." People are just so addicted to spending. Breaking the spending habits starts by creating new, better money habits. When you start making more money, don't change your lifestyle for as long as you can stand it. Start socking it away. If you are tempted to make a major purchase, like a house or a car, always wait at least six months. See if you still want or need it; make no impulse buys.

I stayed in that little six-hundred-square-foot single apartment until my income was over $250,000. I waited to buy a home until I had a quarter million dollars cash saved after the down payment. We were so uncomfortable in that tiny apartment, especially because my teenage sister had moved in with us and was sleeping on the couch. When we finally did buy a home, I bought a very modest house, well within our means. After that, I saved even more aggressively.

My next goal was to be debt-free (outside of my mortgage) and have one million in liquid assets before upgrading my lifestyle again. I'm so glad I listened to this counsel I got from a couple different self-made millionaires. Once I hit that goal, I've never really worried about money ever again. When you have cash, you are more confident. My friend, the first $100,000 is the hardest to save. After that, your limiting beliefs about money start to change. Most people are financially illiterate. Educate yourself. Reading this book is a good start, but one of my hopes for you is that you will continue to learn about money and gain more financial peace of mind.

Here are some basics to get you started.

First, you have heard the saying "pay yourself first." I don't. I tithe first. Give away your first 10 percent. This will make you more humble, less greedy, and not so tight with your money. Money will be less and less of a hard thing in your life. I also happen to believe when you tithe happily and willingly, there are some huge blessings attached—financial blessings.

Hear me out. I'm not trying to push religion on you. I'm trying to help you in all the ways I know have contributed to my success.

The scriptures say that there is the law of the tithe. God gives us all that we have, even our life and that breath you just took. Is it too much to ask that we give him back 10 percent? Tithe means a tenth.

When I started out in business, I studied all the great ones. I read books about successful leaders of the past and present. I studied the lives of people like Walt Disney, Abraham Lincoln, and great religious leaders, coaches, and business success stories I admired. I attended seminars and meetings regularly to learn how to be a better person, a better financial professional, and a better leader. I looked for mentors to learn from and actively tried to build relationships with them. The first book I read as a new entrepreneur was *Rich Dad, Poor Dad*. I loved it. Some of my favorite business books were *Think and Grow Rich* by Napoleon Hill, *Cash Flow Quadrant* by Robert Kiyosaki, and *The Magic of Thinking Big* by Dr. David Schwartz.

I learned that one thing that many of the world's wealthiest families do is give away money. The Rockefeller children were taught to always give away their first 10 percent. Likewise, when I learned about the law of the tithe, I was all in. Even though Shawn and I were struggling financially, and most people thought "we couldn't afford it," we began tithing 10 percent of every paycheck. We did that first, even before we paid the rent of our tiny apartment. We had faith that this was the right thing to do.

Within a few months of starting to give away that money, our income went from less than $100,000 combined to mine alone going over $250,000. If you say you can't afford to give away that money, then I say you can't afford not to.

I have a testimony that tithing brings blessings. It's so significant that I know I would be doing you an *injustice* by leaving it out of this book, just because I was worried someone may get offended. I'm even getting so emotional right now as I write this because I

> *Give! Just 10 percent, it doesn't need to be any more. But it needs to be done with an attitude of gratitude, not begrudgingly.*

know how much this can help you and your family. The blessings are financial in nature. If you don't believe me, just test it. Give! Just 10 percent, it doesn't need to be any more. But it needs to be done with an attitude of gratitude, not begrudgingly. See what happens! See if a blessing doesn't just pour out upon you in a way you can't deny it. If you don't go to church, and you are not sure how to tithe, then just start by giving 10 percent to a charity you love.

Learn to pay yourself next. Honestly, at first it can just be in a savings account. Just start saving a fixed percentage of your paycheck before paying the bills. If you have to cut back on your expenses, do it. Cut the cable, the overpriced coffee, or some other luxury that is costing you your dream future. Once you have paid tithing, taxes, and savings, then you can pay all your other bills. You can finally spend what is left over at the end.

Keep looking for ways to cut back. Maybe there's a less expensive water delivery service or a discount on your cell phone bill, or you can look around for lower costs on your insurance. You can download a free app that helps you get organized and set up a budget. The average family should have at least three to six months of liquid savings in case of emergency. This is usually good advice I give people, but you are not trying to live an *average* life. I want you to have more than that. I want you to have a seriously high cash reserve.

Next is debt. Stacks of liabilities and the overshadowing gloom of debt is modern-day slavery. Don't let yourself be shackled by this unforgiving taskmaster. Get a plan in place quickly to become completely debt-free. There is such a thing as good debt, to some degree. Student loans or owning a home and having a very low mortgage rate can be considered good debt, for now. Eventually, you want a paid-off home as well. Don't let anyone tell you it's better to keep a mortgage. Having no debt is always best. If you have a lot of credit card balances, then let's get a plan in place to get rid of it and never go into debt again. Most people with debt just throw money at the cards each time a bill comes in. There is no plan, and sometimes they are only making minimum payments. This is what the credit card companies hope you do.

All right, here are some tips to becoming debt-free. First, call all your creditors and ask them what your high credit limit is. Find out your balance you owe, and ask them for a lower rate. It doesn't hurt to ask, and you would be surprised how many credit card companies will give you special offers if you haven't made late payments. Make a list of all the cards, the limits, how much you usually pay on each one, the balances, and the rates. As much as possible, move your high-rate balances down to the lower-rate cards if you have room on them. Get as much of the debt to lower interest rates as you can.

Next, figure out how much total money you can allocate toward this monthly debt payment each month.

Let's say that amount is $500 a month. When you make your monthly payments, pay the minimums on all accounts except the highest interest rate card. Put the remaining amount of the $500 toward the balance with the highest interest rate. This may sound unusual, but you want to pay down those high-rate balances first.

Once that card is paid off, don't go spend that money on a new car upgrade. Take the money you were paying on that high-rate card and apply it to the next highest rate card. Keep doing this. When one card is paid off, you roll it down to the next card until eventually you are paying $500 toward the last, lowest interest rate card. Once it's finally paid off and you are debt-free, then you can go buy a new car, right? *Wrong*! Then you start saving for the long term.

The other basic steps to financial independence are saving for your retirement and having the proper insurance in place. I recommend seeking professional guidance on these important matters instead of trying to do it yourself. Find someone who is properly licensed whom you trust. Asking around for referrals is a good place to start. Then do your research to find someone you like. Don't just have someone tell you what to do; have them teach you so that you can teach your children. Break the cycle of financial illiteracy. Learn about compound interest and how your money can work for you. Learn how the different retirement vehicles work and how taxes on the back end can affect your savings. Remember, it's not just how much you save but how much you keep.

The proper amount and right kind of life insurance are important as well. In the two decades I have spent in the financial field, it's been rare that I have worked with a family that understood their life insurance plan. If I had to guess, I would say 98 percent of people I've met with didn't have the proper coverage nor did they understand what they had in place.

Last, protect all that you have worked so hard to build. Having an estate plan, living trust, and will are so important. For an estate plan, again, go to a professional—an established, reputable estate planning attorney whom you like and trust. I also recommend you have a good CPA; it's tempting to do a 1-800-taxes thing or to have a family member help you do your taxes for free, but I can't emphasize enough how much hassle and money you can save by working with an experienced professional.

The last thing I will tell you is this: in every business and life plan you ever create, make sure there are monthly and annual savings goals. Consider also making a savings goal chart, something you see every day. Maybe it's a thermometer that has the date you start saving money at the bottom. At the top, you put the savings goal you desire. It would have the amount of money and the date you wish to acquire it. I thought it would take forever to save that first million dollars in cash. I put a chart up on the wall in my office. Every time I sat down, it was there, eye level to me. My subconscious was being programmed for success in this area every time I was working.

In every business and life plan you ever create, make sure there are monthly and annual savings goals.

Each month, I would fill in my thermometer with the amount of money I had saved plus any interest my accounts had made. I would make a little mark and write my total and the date. As months went by, it grew faster and faster. I still remember pulling it off the wall that last time and sitting there with Shawn as we filled up the chart all the way to the top. We still hadn't upgraded our lifestyle too much. To this day, we live well below our means. Our kids go to great schools, we live in our dream home, and drive nice cars, but we save and save and save. We save more than 50 percent of our income just on the automatic payments alone.

My friend, please make it a mission to get your house in order financially. That way, when the storms of life are crashing outside, you and your family have peace of mind with your safe shelter. The way to build wealth is, first, stop borrowing! Stop spending every-thing you make and trying to impress others. Become completely debt-free. Next, learn to save and pay yourself first. Then, learn to be an investor. Alright, alright, enough with this boring stuff. It had to be included, though, if you really want to win long term. I hope to hear from you someday when you have the big savings and peace of mind and have created all of the happiness you desire. You are building your story. Build it to last, my friend.

The next chapter is the one you have been waiting for: balance! How do you do it all?

Before you begin, though, complete the following action step for this chapter.

ACTION STEP

Create a savings goal chart. Make sure you have a dollar amount and date to achieve it. Write down any ideas that come to mind about creating new money habits.

_____

_____

_____

_____

_____

_____

_____

_____

_____

_____

_____

_____

15

THE JUGGLING ACT

Never get so busy making a living that you forget to make a life.

DOLLY PARTON

Do you sometimes feel as though you're running around like a chicken with its head cut off?

Back in Montana, a friend's grandma cut off a chicken's head right in front of me. Oh, my gosh! I completely freaked out. I was probably five years old. No warning at all.

I was playing with my friends, running around the swing set, when this heavyset, frumpy, angry-looking elderly woman started walking toward us. She looked scary enough in that old, worn-out nightgown, but the squawking chicken sounds made me freeze. She had the hen gripped tight in her plump fist. Before I could even feel sorry for the chicken, who was making a huge scene, the gruff old lady threw that chicken down hard on a stump. Whack! Quickly, she chopped off the head. The dead, headless chicken kept moving around! My friend's eyes almost popped out of his head. Blood was squirting out of its neck. This is where that phrase "like a chicken with its head cut off" came from. A chicken can still jerk around for a few minutes, even after the head is gone.

I think it was the most terrifying thing that had happened to me in life up to that point. Yuck. I felt like I might throw up but just screamed at the top of my lungs as I ran all the way home. I even had a few nightmares over it. I may not feel like a chicken with its head cut off, but I do feel like a frenzied, disorganized hot mess a lot of the time. Many years ago, I was speaking on stage at a large leadership meeting for a few thousand people. Afterward, the host of the meeting asked if a few of the other speakers and I could serve as an expert panel and answer questions from the audience. About halfway through, a woman from the audience stood up. She explained how she felt like she was running around like crazy all the time. "How do you balance it all?" she asked. "I have three kids and don't know how to fit it all in."

No one wants to feel overstretched, exasperated, and stressed all the time.

One of the other women on the panel answered first. She's a hard worker, a mom, and someone I genuinely respect. I was surprised at her response.

"It's total chaos all the time, but you just have to make it happen," she said. "I'm running around like crazy, trying to find a clean baby bottle and grab something to eat. Get less sleep if you have to. It sucks right now. I never have time for myself, but that's OK. I'm always stressed, but it's worth it."

I don't think it was the answer this poor lady wanted to hear.

I was shocked, so I jumped in.

"I personally don't like chaos, and when I'm a stressed-out mess, I'm not effective as a leader or as a mom," I answered. I went on to give her practical advice to help her gain some stability and structure to her daily routine.

No one wants to feel overstretched, exasperated, and stressed all the time. That other female speaker who had given the first answer found herself sick a few years later because of stress and not taking good care of herself. She even stepped away from her business for a little while because of burnout. I want to help you avoid this happening to you.

What was the advice I gave to that mom entrepreneur about balance? Before I answer that, let me just say I'm probably the busiest person I know. I'm up by 7:00 a.m. every day, usually earlier. My high schooler attends a church class before school, so sometimes I'm up way earlier to make sure she is ready to go. The morning is nuts getting four kids ready for school and out the door on time with lunches and teeth brushed. I try to get in a workout daily, so I have to carve out time for that, usually in the morning. I have calls to return, appointments to do, clients to see, and meetings to run. There are after-school pickups, sports practices, grocery shopping, church youth activities, and the "Mom, can my friends come over?" happening daily.

Sometimes there will be two or even three kids' sports events going on at the same time in different parts of town. That's always fun. Then there is also the occasional birthday party, drivers ed training, parent-teacher conference, pediatrician check-up, piano recital, band performance, and Pinewood Derby, most of which usually require me to bring something like a present, an activity, or a treat. Of course, I have the desire to do daily scripture study, personal development reading, and self-care. How about finding the time to get a haircut or maybe your nails done once in a while, not to mention trying to schedule a personal doctor's appointment. This would be hard for anyone to make happen. This crazy schedule is a lot for a stay-at-home mom to juggle, let alone someone running a company with thousands of associates needing my attention as well.

Let me explain how it all gets done. First of all, it doesn't always all get done, and that's OK. I drop the ball sometimes too. A couple of years ago, when Benny was in preschool, it was a particularly crazy morning. I got the big kids dropped off right before the bell rang.

Benny had dressed himself because I was too busy making lunches last minute. We rushed out the door as I noticed he was wearing a Flash (the superhero) costume and his big brother's cowboy boots. His hair was total bedhead, and he had the biggest smile across his face. He looked awesome. It was either go back inside and change, which would make everyone late for school—the big boys would not be happy with a tardy that wasn't their fault—or just let him go to school like that. It was only preschool, so I thought, *What the heck, his shoes are too big, but it won't hurt anything.* All the other kids were already in the class as we walked up the path to his school.

As we approached the front door Benny said, "Mommy, I'm so excited it's Picture Day today."

"No, it's not," I said quickly. When I got in the class and was signing him in, I asked the teacher if it was, in fact, Picture Day. Sure was! *I don't remember getting an email on this,* I thought. I started getting mad at the teacher, as if this was somehow her fault and not mine.

We rushed home, and I changed his clothes as fast as I could, combed his hair as best I could, and rushed back right in time for him to make his class picture. His still messy hair and wrinkled shirt were way better than cowboy Flash. Wow! Good job,

Supermom! Stuff like this has happened to us all. The key is to just laugh when it happens. Something like this happened when Daisy was little too. I forgot that it was "Show and Tell" day at school. I dropped her off without something to show. Man, did I beat myself up about that. I remember how bad I felt when I walked back to the car, thinking I was the worst mom in the world. As if forgetting to bring a stuffed animal to kindergarten was going to ruin my kid forever. First-child drama! Now, I know it's not a bad mom thing; it's a human being thing. Cut yourself some slack.

More recently, I showed up to a birthday party for a five-year-old girl named Sofia. We brought the cutest little sparkly unicorn backpack as a gift. When Benny and I arrived, he ran quickly to the superhero bounce house and started playing with his friends. I put the gift on the table and started talking with the other parents. It didn't take me long to realize that the birthday party was for a completely different friend named Dylan, and he wasn't into pink unicorns. How the heck did I screw that up? I had to run a quick covert operation and have Shawn run by the store to pick up a new gift, wrap it, and drop it off to me at the park before it was time to open gifts. As slick as possible, I walked by the gift table and grabbed my pretty present with the shiny, pink bow. Hoping none of the other parents noticed, I slid it under my shirt and walked it casually to my car. And the Mom of the Year goes to .... *not me!* Again, I just have to laugh, not stress.

It's OK to make mistakes; we are all human. It's also OK not to do it all. You don't have to always bake the cookies yourself. Cookies from the grocery store's bakery are an easy solution when you have too much on your plate. You can also ask for help. Make a list of all the family and friends who love you and love your kids. Maybe a parent, a best friend, or relative can help with drop-offs or carpool. Maybe you can ask your sister to pick up that birthday gift for you since she is making a Target run. Maybe there is a friend in the neighborhood who has kids around your kids' age whom you can make a deal with. She watches your kids while you do some business errands, and you can watch her kids when she has to take her mom to the doctor.

Get creative and resourceful, and most importantly learn to have a sense of humor when you completely drop the ball. You may have many roles. Some are more important than others. Do you remember earlier when I discussed the importance of knowing your priorities? That will come into play a lot here. I want you to identify all your roles. For example, I'm a wife and a mother, but I'm also a daughter, sister, and friend. I'm a business leader and a Sunday school teacher. These are some of my more important roles. I want to make sure I'm not neglecting any of my major roles in life, and as you can see, there are a lot.

This is why if someone asks me to take on a new project, I am very careful. If I'm going to add something to my plate, I have to be willing to take something else off. I don't want to try to do more than I can handle. Learn to say *no!* For some, this is not so easy. The people pleasers never want to disappoint, so they tend to agree to things they don't want to do. Then they become overwhelmed and unhappy. You don't have to be rude or abrupt. Part of self-care is setting boundaries. It's OK and healthy to say no to things that don't fit on your current plate. You can politely decline.

I was once asked to be the head of the PTA. Yikes. My gut response was, "Heck no. No way. No thank you. Absolutely not!" Instead, I politely said, "Wow, I am honored that you would even think of me for such a substantial role. Let me talk it over with my husband, and I will get back to you." I have a script for things like this.

I then sent an email saying again how nice it was for them to ask me and I was honored, but my husband thought I had too much on my plate at that time. Which was true because he always thinks I have too much on my plate. I then went on to say, "I'd be happy to help where I can throughout the year; please let me know where I can be involved as events come up."

You see; you *can* say no in a nice way. If you have guilty feelings on things like this, "Let it goooo! Let it goooo!" It's really not as big of a deal as you think it is. I promise you, they will find someone to do it. As much as I love my kids, being the head of the PTA won't make them any happier, and it will just add more to my already packed plate. Define your most important roles and priorities. This will make it so much easier to say no to things that create new, unimportant, unnecessary roles and responsibilities in the future.

Once you have identified the important goals, tasks, and people in your life, then you can allocate your time properly. If not, then you are just reacting all the time to whatever is going on around you. As urgent matters come up, you more than likely focus your attention there. You are like a ship being tossed around on the waves as strong winds blow you in all directions. It's exhausting and wastes a lot of time as you are trying to tend to one thing when the next pops up before you're ready. There will always be the occasional emergency, but don't treat every day like this, reacting to what needs to be handled.

Have you ever looked at the clock and wondered, "What happened to my day? I haven't finished anything that I wanted to." We've all been there. Instead, be more intentional with your time. After all, it is such a precious resource that you can never get back. Your time is so valuable, even the ten minutes of one-on-one time you have with a child can mean so much in their life. The eight-minute pep talk that you have with one of your teammates that encourages them not to give up can change their family's whole life. What you choose to spend your time on really can determine your future. So many people are casual in how they spend their days, and the result is so much wasted time. I'm often surprised that I get done in a day what someone else may get done in two or three days. It's not that I am better than them; I'm just more intentional with my time.

Don't get me wrong. I'm not an "all work and no play" type of person. I really do have an amazingly fun life. I wanted more than just fun though. I wanted to create my dream life, a fulfilling life of passion and service and contribution. In order to get it all in, you have to be more proactive than reactive. A little bit of planning and time management go a long way. It may sound boring and not spontaneous and fun, but trust me, going to Hawaii every year *is* fun. Traveling the world with your spouse *is* fun. Being able to help out your family anytime they need you *is* fun. Being stressed out because you are always reacting to what gets thrown at you is not so fun.

What you choose to spend your time on really can determine your future.

Here's how you plan it all in. First, use some form of planner or calendar. I know you may prefer using your phone or some device to store appointments, but I encourage you to at least get a big household calendar that the whole family can see. Keep it somewhere like the kitchen or family room. Maybe each family member has their activities written in a different color. I'm not that organized, but I have friends who have done this, and it works for them. I do, however, still use a paper planner. I like to be able to see on paper everything at a glance for the week, the month, and the year. I get asked all the time about which planner I recommend. I've searched for the perfect agenda/calendar and still haven't found it yet. Maybe someday I will just create my own. The ones I tend to like the best are the ones that have the month and the weeks laid out. I want to open it up and see the whole week I am on and have plenty of room to write appointments in on each day. There are some cute ones out there that have space for to-do lists and habit trackers that I like as well. Just try different versions until you have one that suits you.

Planning ahead helps me a lot. Scrambling last minute always causes anxiety. Would you rather be planning or reacting? By preplanning my day the night before, there are way less last-minute stressors. You can also preplan your week. You know all that lame stuff you do each day that wastes time? The things that are not very urgent but are still somewhat important and have to get done. Things like updating records or going through unopened mail. How about scheduling an hour a week to work on those things and get caught up on them?

Planning ahead can also save you money. For example, I know the kids will have spring break this year. I can plan it now, months in advance, and get way better deals if we want to go somewhere. Put your priorities on your calendar first, then schedule around them.

At the beginning of each quarter, I put the bigger events on the calendar, like the company conventions that I can't miss or family vacations we already have planned. Remember, your heart is where you decide to spend your time. If I truly do have my priorities of faith, family, and then business, then I would plan my time accordingly. For faith, I try to plan in service days once a quarter, and I set aside Sundays for my church activities.

Next, I put in a mini honeymoon each quarter. My marriage is my most primary role, so that goes into my calendar next. Can I just remind you right here to make the time for your self-care? Don't forget to put the appointment with yourself on the calendar. At the beginning of each month, I schedule in a family day, family members' birthdays, and important things like playoff games, school performances, and mommy dates. During our weekly family councils, we all talk about any upcoming events or items that need to be added to the family calendar. This also prevents the kids from asking me to help with a school project or bake brownies the night before. Doesn't that drive you nuts? If it's not on the calendar, it's not happening. This rule is super helpful for my stress levels. Happy & Strong!

I know this sounds so boring. Unless you are a freak like me who likes to plan, it's not that exciting. It is worth it though. Preparation is a trait of all champions. I will warn, however, against excessive planning. Just like excessive busyness leads to stress and agitation, excessive planning leads to not being flexible. You have to remain open to changes in your schedule and your time structure. If you are too rigid, you miss out on the fun and spontaneous joys in life. If you make to-do lists, prioritize them. Ask yourself, what is the most important thing I need to do today? This week? Do the most important things first and be OK with the fact that you can't do it all sometimes.

Ask yourself, what is the most important thing I need to do today? This week? Do the most important things first and be OK with the fact that you can't do it all sometimes.

My kids each have their own planners that they can bring to the family council meetings. We talk about upcoming events on the calendar that might be important to them. If there are conflicting events, like maybe Austin has a baseball game at the same time Daisy has a band performance, then we talk about possible solutions. Maybe I go to one event and Shawn goes to another. There have been times when Shawn and I had an important business meeting that we felt both of us should attend. We would have to miss an important sports event or something that one of the kids had. Again, we would talk about it as a family and come up with a solution. Maybe Grandpa or Uncle Jeremy can come watch. If Uncle Me-Me (their nickname for their beloved Uncle Jeremy) could go to a game, it really didn't matter where mom and dad were. If Me-Me is involved, mom and dad are chopped liver. Once in a while, one of the kids will express the desire for the whole family's support. "Who's coming to my presentation next week?" Brody asked in a family council meeting. "Can Austin get out of class for a few minutes? Maybe you could ask the school to sign him out, Mom. I will ask my teacher if Benny can come too." He was doing a verbal report on Henry Ford but doing the whole thing using an English accent. You can see why he was so excited to have as many of us there as possible. Family council is such *a huge* part of why our busy family can stay somewhat organized and sane.

All the important stuff for each family member is on the calendar.

The late Stephen Covey once said, "The key is in not spending time but in investing it." He wrote many great books, including *First Things First* and his *Seven Habits* books. I saw Mr. Covey give a great talk years ago. You might have seen this example before, but it won't hurt to be reminded of this valuable learning moment. In his speech, he did an object lesson. He had a bucket full of big rocks and a bucket of sand. Mr. Covey asked someone to try to fit the contents of both buckets in a glass container.

The volunteer dumped the sand in first and then found it pretty impossible to try to shove all the big rocks into the full canister. Then after emptying the glass container, he instead put all the big rocks in first, then poured in the sand. The sand found its way through the spaces between the rocks and completely filled the container. It was a great visual.

The big rocks represented all the most important things in life, like family and health. If you put those in first, everything else fills in around it. If you initially plan all the important stuff into your calendar, then you can absolutely max out the rest of your schedule. You can fill in all the gaps, working or doing whatever you have to do to win in life and business. You also won't feel guilty when you are working because you are probably spending more time with your kids and spouse than most people do.

There is no such thing as perfect balance, only *striving* for balance and happiness. The idea of reaching and keeping balance all the time is a lie. Ralph Waldo Emerson said, "For everything you gain, you lose something." There will be times that you are going for a major business goal and you are way off balance, tipping the scale more toward financials and career. There may be other times in your life where a family member is sick or a child is struggling in school or with other challenges. Then you are off balance the other direction, spending more time with the family. Use your common sense, gut instinct, and heart to tell you what is best *right now* and for the long term for your family.

I can't express enough how important it is to *communicate*. Communication with your family and any other support person you have is critical. We have those weekly family councils, but the kids know they can talk about anything with us at any time. Shawn and I are going over the schedules daily, changing things as new situations come up. We are both fluid and flexible.

"I was supposed to do this leadership meeting next Thursday, but now Austin has his student of the month presentation at school that day. Can you run the meeting?" or "My appointment rescheduled; I can pick up the kids tomorrow." I call it CPC, constant personal communication. It's brief but effective. It might take only a minute as I'm changing for bed or as we are eating lunch. We always do it in our partners' meetings.

The Apollo rockets made it to the moon, but they were off course 97 percent of the time. That means for every half hour the ship was in flight, it was on course for less than sixty seconds. The rockets needed constant course correction by communication with Houston. They still reached their destination and landed on the moon with precision and perfect timing. Constant personal communication is key. I'm crystal clear on my destination. I may be off course most of the time, but Shawn and I are touching base and doing constant course correction daily.

The last thing I have to add is *simplify*. If there is any way to declutter, reduce, or cut back some part of your overly complex life, do it. Simplify to multiply! What are you trying to multiply? Your results, your prosperity, your time, and your joyfulness. No need to overcomplicate this. You don't have to be the perfect Pinterest parent. I am so far from that. If that makes you happy, then do it. But if it's taking too much time from other, more important priorities you have, then stop. I call it "delegate or dump."

Identify a few things that you can take off that overloaded plate and give to someone else or abandon completely.

Do you have a few roles you have acquired that you need to drop? Are there unnecessary tasks you do that can be delegated? Identify a few things that you can take off that overloaded plate and give to someone else or abandon completely.

Maybe instead of that grocery store run that takes hours out of your week, you can order online and have them delivered. I have a weekly meal plan sheet that I fill out Sunday nights. It makes it easy to order groceries one time on Monday. It used to drive me nuts wasting time making extra grocery store runs. Are you overly involved anywhere? Maybe you can use a crockpot or Instant Pot a few more nights a week.

How about having the kids do their own laundry or setting their clothes out the night before? You could get better at balancing your checking account so all your bills can be put on auto pay and you don't waste time each month on this. What systems could you put in place at work to make it more streamlined and duplicable for others to implement? Get creative and put some thought into this concept of simplifying your life. I am all about simplifying. If it doesn't grow me, my faith, my family, my business, or my health, it doesn't make the cut. It doesn't belong on my plate.

Zig Ziglar said, "You can't truly be considered successful in your business life if your home life is in shambles." Strive for balance and you *can* build the ideal life for you and your family. I want you to create a dream life, a life you don't feel you need to take a vacation from. A life that you can't wait to wake up in the morning and experience. First build it in your mind, then build it on paper, then go build it! What I mean by this is paint a vivid picture in your mind of what you want for you and your family. Then write it out on paper. Create goals and deadlines and put as much passion, enthusiasm, and imagination into it as possible. You design it in your imagination first, create the blueprints, then go build it. Take continuous, persistent action toward where you want to be. Shawn and I think back on all the times we sat to talk and dream of the life we have today. Don't settle; go after the life you desire. Instead of always worrying about being off balance, focus on moving closer to your vision and make sure you keep growing happier and stronger as an individual and as a family.

I can't wait for what's coming next. I know we talked about making more time for yourself, but it's also important to make time for others. It's probably my favorite part of MY Happy & Strong vision. It's also one of the single most effective ways to keep you and your business growing long term.

Before you move on to the next chapter, take a few minutes to complete the action step on the next page.

ACTION STEP

What are some ways you can simplify your life? Who would love to help you more often? Write down any ideas that came up as you read this chapter.

_____

_____

_____

_____

_____

_____

_____

_____

_____

_____

_____

16

Focus on Others

The best way to find yourself is to lose yourself in the service of others.

Mahatma Gandhi

My friend Johanna and I were nervously holding hands in the doctor's office, trying to support each other. We went together so neither one of us would chicken out. The doctor had just told us we were getting eight vaccines that day. That wasn't happening.

"Uh, no! I will take the yellow fever shot and give me something for malaria, please."

I hate vaccines, and I sure wasn't getting eight of them. We explained to the doctor that all we needed was what was required to get past customs in Africa. He tried to explained how it's only a one in over a million chance of any type of bad reaction.

"My husband was that one in a million," Johanna answered back. "When he was two years old, he received a DPT vaccine that was a bad batch, and he was crippled on the right side of his body. He has cerebral palsy and can't use his right hand."

Neither one of us was willing to let them give us all those vaccines, not ever, but especially not all in one day.

"Will you be around the native people while you're there?" the doctor asked. "If so, you should at least get the vaccine for meningitis, so you won't be worried every time someone coughs or sneezes."

> *If all your goals are only about you and your family, then eventually you will reach your goals and stop growing.*

We definitely were going to be around the people. I, for one, didn't want to worry about dying every time a child had a sniffly nose, so we got the additional shot and a few weeks later were on our way to a small orphanage in Kampala.

By now, I think you know me well enough to know I'll tell you like it is and not leave something out that isn't really important to your happiness. I'm going to give you one last thing to add to that plate of yours (as if you didn't have enough to do already, right?). This is a big one in your overall sense of well-being and fulfillment. I hope by now you have clarity on what you want your life to look like. I hope you have it all written out with plans on how you will make it happen.

You can visualize all the great places you will travel, the home you will live in, sending your kids to fantastic schools, and maybe even some fun goals like taking a gourmet cooking class in Italy, learning a foreign language, and driving an exotic car. Having clarity on what you want is key. However, if all your goals are only about you and your family, then eventually you will reach your goals and stop growing. I want to challenge you to have some contribution goals. Not only does this cause you to keep thinking bigger and personally growing, but it also brings you more fulfillment and joy along the way. Mahatma Gandhi said, "The best way to find yourself is to lose yourself in the service of others."

You may be thinking, *Jaime, you already asked me to give away 10 percent of my income. What else are you talking about here?*

I'm talking about your legacy. What impact will your life make? Marie Osmond declared, "Being of service to others is what brings true happiness." I am involved in several charitable causes and have spent countless hours and dollars on things I love. It doesn't make me any better than anyone else, but it does make me happier. One of my favorite trips was that trip with my friends to Kampala, Uganda, in Africa. The All For One Foundation where I serve on the board builds prosperity centers for children. These are basically orphanages that also serve as a school and medical center. The one in Kampala is very special to me. My team and I had helped build it many years ago by throwing one of our famous fundraising costume parties. Thirteen years later, we wanted to go visit in person because we were starting a project to build a cafeteria, more classrooms, an additional dorm, and a full medical clinic.

I sat on the floor with a full heart as the kids just waited to give me hugs. These orphans just wanted to be touched and hugged, and they patiently waited for their turn to be squeezed. My joy was overflowing, and tears ran down my face every time they danced together or I heard their beautiful voices sing. I know that trip changed me as a person. I'm definitely better in every role I play in life because I decided to put my busy schedule on hold, spend my own money to fly across the world, and just love on these beautiful little people I had never met before.

What do you want to be known for after you are gone? I want my posterity to always remember me as the one who changed our family's legacy. The direction of our family tree will be forever changed because Shawn and I worked hard and made it happen. But I don't just want to help my family. I want to really leave my mark on this world long after I am gone. I have so many things I am passionate about: autism, wellness and education for children in third world countries, childhood schizophrenia, refugee families starting their lives over here in the US, human trafficking (especially child trafficking), the suicide rate of our veterans, battered women and children…there are just so many things that need our attention and help. Explore what pulls at your heart strings. What makes you really passionate or really pissed off? What injustices need to be corrected? Light yourself on fire with a crusade to serve others. You can make a difference, and you are more potent as a leader in business and in your home when you are ignited with a desire to make an impact.

I am not just a go-getter; I want to be a *go-giver*! Lifting others and being involved in charity work is a huge part of a Happy & Strong life. As much as I have emphasized making time for yourself, it's also important to make time for others. You don't have to wait until you are rich to start either. It could be as simple as planting trees and flowers with your kids to make your neighborhood more beautiful. It could be doing a service project as a family to rake leaves and clean up the yard of a widow you know. Doing service gets you to stop worrying, fretting, and focusing on what's going wrong in your life. Charity is showing pure love, putting others first, and it makes you a more humble and happier person. Research has also shown that spending money on others brings more happiness than spending money on yourself. I guess the old saying "It's better to give than receive" is actually true. Buying material things for yourself brings only so much pleasure, and it's not long lasting. Studies on this subject have shown it doesn't take a large amount of money to make a difference. It was interesting that happiness levels of the giver were boosted even with just five dollars or twenty-dollar gifts.

For Christmas, I used to buy the kids so many gifts. Instead, I now give them opportunities to earn extra money. I take them individually shopping to buy their family members gifts with their own money. They love doing this and are so thoughtful as they pick out presents for their siblings. Our Christmas morning is way more joyful with this new tradition.

Remember, *your kids are watching.* Daisy is always doing service projects, sometimes with her church youth group, sometimes through school, and sometimes on her own.

"Mom, for my birthday I'm going to throw the party of the year!" She said this right before turning five years old.

Doing service gets you to stop worrying, fretting, and focusing on what's going wrong in your life.

"OK, what did you have in mind?" I figured she would ask for some elaborate Disney princess–themed party.

"I am going to invite everyone from school, everyone from your work, and everyone from church. It's going to be *huge,*" she explained, as her voice grew louder with excitement. "We will have a Spiderman bounce house because boys and girls all love Spiderman."

She went on and on as I started to laugh.

"I will order some pizza, and you can cut watermelon to eat for the snacks...and at the end, a big piñata."

"Sounds fun," I said. "Where should we have this giant party?"

"At the pumpkin park!"

Do your kids give nicknames to all the local parks? My kids always have. There was the tree park, the pirate park, the dinosaur park, the red park. The "pumpkin park" got its name because there was a big pumpkin festival there every year for Halloween.

"That one has an area for big kids and baby kids!" Her eyes were huge by now. "And that's not even the best part. Do you want to know the best part, Mom?"

"What's the best part, Daisy?" I said as I waited for the next dramatic idea. Back then she never stopped talking. Daisy is smart and creative, and she is like the Energizer bunny, always on the go. I was used to her sharing her grand schemes with me all day long. "I'm going to tell all the kids not to bring any presents. I'm going to tell them to bring a nice old toy or book or maybe a used blanket. Then after the party, we will take all the stuff they bring to the kids who have no daddies."

My heart was so touched, and my eyes started to well up a little. The "kids with no daddies" is what she called the women's shelter that she had seen me donate all their old toys and clothes at least a few times a year. She was only five, but I let her plan that party. She even picked out the watermelons and called to order the bounce house herself. It was a giant party with hundreds of guests. The kids at the park that day had the time of their lives, and afterward we took three truckloads of gifts to two different shelters. I still remember the smile on her face when she hopped out of the truck and grabbed two giant trash bags, one in each hand. They dwarfed her. She was so happy walking into the women's shelter, even happier than when she was playing with all her friends at "the party of the year."

Later, when Daisy was about ten, she knew I organized a charity event every Christmas morning to bring clothes to Skid Row in downtown LA. She asked if there were also homeless children there. When I told her that 40 percent of the homeless population are children and teens, she decided to do a fundraising project to buy Christmas gifts that she would hand out to the homeless youth. She hosted several lemonade stands, sold gratitude rocks, and did a few hot chocolate booths. She raised over $1,200, bought all the presents, and wrapped them herself.

Early Christmas morning before sunrise, we went down to Skid Row and joined many of our friends handing out clothes and food. The kids sang carols from the back of a truck, and Daisy handed out her wrapped presents. She noticed as teens would come crawling out of the tents on the sidewalk they lived in, or a pregnant mom would come up with her child asking if they could have one too. All these experiences touch you in different ways. They make us want to be better, more compassionate, and grow so we can make an even bigger difference.

There is science now that tells us when we lose ourselves in the service of others, we are happier.

My boys love doing "man work" service projects like gardening or painting for the community or a family in need. Again, it can be big or small. Get involved! There is science now that tells us when we lose ourselves in the service of others, we are happier.

Let me give you some simple ideas to try out with your family. How about volunteering at a local school? Think of your talents; maybe you are artistic or good at gardening. If you love baking, maybe make cookies to bring to the senior center or the nurses of a local hospital. There are youth groups and classrooms that could use your help. Maybe visiting a widow or someone who is lonely and just chatting or playing a game of cards. Maybe watching a busy mother's kids for a few hours so she can run errands. The possibilities are endless and don't have to cost a lot of money.

You could make little bags with toiletries and snacks to keep in your car to hand out next time you see a homeless person asking for help. It could be as simple as posting about a charity you love to bring awareness. There is a great website called justserve.org. If you enter your zip code, it will show you all the local charities and causes looking for volunteers. They have options for ongoing service projects and little things that you can do from home in just five minutes. I want to challenge you to find ways to serve often and discover what ignites the passion in you for a long-term contribution goal.

If you liked this lesson, just wait for what I have for you next. I will give you more practical tips on cultivating happiness and one of the biggest and best opportunities to have an incredible leap in personal growth.

Now it's time for you to complete this chapter's action step.

ACTION STEP

Make a list of causes that you are passionate about. What are fun ways to get involved in your community to make a difference?

_____

_____

_____

_____

_____

_____

_____

_____

_____

_____

_____

17

THE SCIENCE OF HAPPINESS

Happiness is not something readymade. It comes from your own actions.

DALAI LAMA

After my uncle molested me, I hated him. Every time I saw him, I was disgusted. I didn't care that he was homeless; I felt he deserved the life he had. He was an alcoholic and would steal my money, my birthday money I was saving up to buy something special, to go buy a six pack of beer.

When he was a younger man, he was driving drunk with a friend late one night through Malibu Canyon. As he sped around one of the sharp curves, he lost control, and the small sedan slammed into the side of the mountain. He and his friend were both crushed in the wreckage. Ronnie was in the hospital for a long time with a back broken in several places. They had to fuse his vertebrae with metal plates that later caused him endless pain. Even more painful than that his good friend who was in the passenger seat that night was left paralyzed from the neck down.

I was a kid. It didn't matter to me that he was drunk; it didn't matter that he was depressed and living miserably. There was no excuse for him to do what he did in that bed that night. For a long time, I would remember exactly how it felt when he touched me, and I would get so angry. Later as an adult, I realized I had still not fully forgiven him. When men would say inappropriate things to me, I would pretend I misunderstood them and walk away instead of standing up for myself.

Aristotle declared, "Happiness depends upon ourselves." The last few winning principles I want you to understand about building a Happy & Strong future are *forgiveness* and *gratitude.*

It's a scientific fact that if you are showing more gratitude, you are a happier person. Also, holding a grudge can breed more anger and sadness. Oprah has a powerful story. She grew up in poverty and suffered hardship and repeated sexual abuse. She was quoted to say, "True forgiveness is when you can say 'thank you' for that experience." I know forgiving can be really hard sometimes, especially when someone has offended you deeply. If it's something little, and maybe the person didn't really mean to hurt you, then just apply the "Let it goooo!" technique. Try not to be offensive but also try not to *be* offended.

In other more severe cases, where someone intentionally hurt you, it may be harder to forgive. For example, the drunk driver who hit a child you love, the rapist who hurt you or a loved one, an abusive adult in your life when you were a child, or a significant other who cheated on you and broke your heart. All these acts can be so hard to forgive, but holding a grudge doesn't usually hurt the other person—it just keeps cutting *you* deeper. It's like a sore that you keep picking at and not allowing to finally just heal. If you truly want to live a life of abundance, wealth, and happiness, forgiveness will help these things flow more freely into your life.

Ralph Waldo Emerson said, "For every minute you are angry, you lose sixty seconds of happiness." When you forgive someone, it doesn't mean you have to be friends with that person; you don't have to like them, and it doesn't mean that what they did is OK. I believe it's not my place to judge others. Everyone will have the law of the harvest come back around to them. If they are truly a bad person, then they will eventually get what they deserve, with or without my festering anger toward them.

If you truly want to live a life of abundance, wealth, and happiness, forgiveness will help these things flow more freely into your life.

When I learned the value of forgiveness and the blessings of happiness it brings, I decided to just let it go and completely forgive my uncle. It did not make what he did OK. I didn't have to be his buddy. Sometimes you just have to let relationships end. I never once let my kids be around him, but once I truly forgave him, I had so much more peace and happiness opened up to me. I also gained empathy toward Ronnie. I felt sorry for him. This happens a lot when you forgive. The resentment melts away and is replaced with compassion sometimes. As I mentioned earlier in the book, Ronnie was badly abused. When he was nine years old, he started a fire in the neighborhood. My grandpa punished him by holding his hands in the hot flames on their kitchen stove.

"Do you want to play with fire?" he shouted. "Let's play with some fire here and see how you like it!"

Ronnie suffered severe burns. When his injuries finally healed, he was placed in a home for incorrigible boys until he turned eighteen. How sad that this little boy's parents gave up on him. Finally, I saw him as a person again instead of as a monster. The law of the harvest did come around to my uncle; he died painfully of throat cancer, homeless and alone. I'm sure he had a heart full of guilt.

Do yourself a favor, my friend, and let go of any grudges you may be holding. Letting go of a grudge is not just about being compassionate. It's about self-care. Consider calling the person you have not yet forgiven. Make the effort; maybe even write it in a letter. Even if you never send the letter, you will feel better. Not forgiving someone breeds resentment and feelings of revenge. It causes unwanted stress. Studies show forgiving improves your physical abilities and helps you live a longer life. When I forgive someone, it helps me more than them. Nowadays, I have learned to forgive almost immediately. I can't even hold a grudge more than a few hours. It doesn't mean I don't get upset; I just don't let it fester and steal my joy. Forgiveness is a secret to a happy life. Take a step right now to forgive.

Being grateful and showing gratitude is another way to live a happier and stronger life. There always are so many things we can be grateful for if we look for them. I'm grateful for my body and that it's working properly. Since giving birth to my first child, the human body has been a marvel to me. I'm grateful I live at this time, in such a modern world. We have so many books, conveniences, technology, and modern medicine. With the touch of an app, we can have a car pick us up or food at our door in no time. I'm grateful for my family, friends, and colleagues who have supported me and made me who I am today. I'm so grateful for the beauty of the world we live in. I love nature and what it provides for us. I can enjoy the snow with my children and also watch them splash at the beach. I'm grateful for all I have and all the lessons I endured. I'm most grateful to my Father in heaven, for His love and mercy. We are truly blessed. Shouldn't we express our gratitude a lot more often?

Studies have proven that one of the greatest contributing factors to overall happiness in your life is how much gratitude you show. One experiment had a group of people take a test. They answered a series of questions to determine their happiness level. They had no idea what the test was designed to measure. Afterward, they were asked to think of someone they were thankful for. Someone like a parent, friend, or mentor that they really appreciated because that person had made such an impact on their life. Next, they had to write down as much as they could about that person and why they were so grateful for them. Last, they were asked to pick up the phone and call the person they were grateful for and read them what they wrote. They were asked to not just feel grateful but also express their gratitude out loud.

After the calls were made, the test was given again. The questions were mixed up and rephrased so as not to let on that they were taking the same test twice. The results were amazing. Every person was happier after having the feelings of gratitude. The people who actually got to talk to their friend on the phone and express those feelings showed an instant increase in happiness levels. The increase in happiness was anywhere between 4 and 19 percent. Another interesting fact about this experiment was that the person who experienced the biggest jump in happiness was the least happy person in the group to start. Isn't that awesome? You can google a short video on it called "An Experiment in Gratitude / The Science of Happiness." You will love it.

One simple way to add more joy into your life (who couldn't use a little more of that?) is by starting a gratitude journal. I keep one by my bed, and even though I don't use it every night, I write in it often. I try to think of at least three things I'm grateful for each day. It helps me recall the miracles among the chaos.

Even if the kids were like wild beasts that day, I may recall a funny look Benny gave me that made me smile or when Shawn gave me a hug in the kitchen. I might be grateful for the new chocolate I found at Whole Foods or that Austin cleaned the kitchen without being asked. There is always something to be grateful for if you look for it. Another idea is writing a handwritten letter or card to someone thanking them. Maybe a mom in the neighborhood who always looks out for the kids, a teacher who made a difference for you or one of your children, or a business mentor who sets a good example for you to follow. Acts of kindness and gratitude rarely cost much time or money, but they pay huge dividends back into your emotional bank account.

One simple way to add more joy into your life (who couldn't use a little more of that?) is by starting a gratitude journal.

Another idea is to set an alert on your phone that reminds you to think about what you are grateful for. Gratitude breeds higher life satisfaction.

I am now a student of the science of happiness. What creates more feelings of well-being and joy? Let me give you a few last tips. First, smile and laugh more. Sometimes you have to fake it till you make it. Even if you are not feeling good, smile. Surprisingly, this helps. Sometimes I will be driving in my car and I will just make myself laugh hard, out loud. It doesn't take long before I'm actually smiling and laughing without it being forced. People might think you are crazy, but it works.

Spend more time with friends and family. One of the top five regrets people on their death bed have is always that they didn't spend enough time with loved ones. Schedule time to call distant family members and reconnect with old friends. When you are having family time, try to put down your phone and really be present.

Speaking of putting down the phone, another happiness tip is to unplug once in a while. Completely disconnect and go on a social media fast for a couple of weeks. When you return to it, stop following anyone who posts things that make you feel angry or afraid in any way. I know we talked about not being on your device before bed, but it's also not good to get on social media or any devices first thing in the morning.

Have a solid morning routine to start your day right, focused on positives. Start adjusting your schedule to get up a little earlier and establishing great habits. A great morning routine is the foundation of your self-care practice. It will make a big difference in your mental well-being and set the pace for a happier, more productive day. Everyone is different, so experiment with some various practices to see what works best for you.

No matter what your morning routine is, put off looking at your phone until later. In fact, keep it in another room. Here are a few ideas to try out. I already told you I start my day with a glass of water. I have heard lots of people say to make your bed first thing. To be totally honest, this doesn't usually happen right away for me. I can be messy like that. Don't judge. I do have to brush my teeth right away though. I feel gross if I don't. Next, maybe prayer or meditation. Take some time to just be still. You could visualize having little successes throughout your day.

If you are a morning person, exercise can be great as part of your routine. If not, how about at least stretching your body and getting the blood flowing? I also like to read my goals and affirmations and write in my journal. I love to get up while it's still a little dark out before any of the kids are up. It's the only time the house is completely quiet and peaceful. With a cozy blanket and a cup of mint or buckwheat tea, I sit with my scriptures and my journal. Journaling brings clarity and peace to my mind. The journal entry might be about areas I feel I need to improve. I try to remember blessings and tender mercies that I experienced that week. It could be taking notes on a book I'm reading or a passage of scripture that morning. I write down all the things I have to get done, look at my planner, ponder on which things are *most* important, and say another prayer. By identifying the most important tasks to get done, you will feel far less reactive as your day unfolds.

Starting the day by prioritizing people over tasks or things will lead to a much healthier lifestyle.

I practice gratitude by writing at least one thing I appreciate about my husband and each of my children. I also eat a nutritious breakfast or at the very least, a smoothie. The fuel you take in each morning will give you the energy to perform. I know there will be some busy mornings and you will be rushing to get out of the house. Don't skip it. Your body has been fasting in your sleep, and it needs that vital kick start. It will also help with your metabolism; who doesn't want that? I also recommend that you sit down with your family to eat breakfast whenever possible. Starting the day by prioritizing people over tasks or things will lead to a much healthier lifestyle.

Create your ideal schedule by doing a few focused things each day. Don't feel like you have to completely change your morning routine all at once. Try adding in a new practice each week and take note of improvements. Eventually, you will figure out what makes you the happiest and productive. Your personal regimen should make you feel energized about your day and ultimately your life. It also will generate more self-discipline. The worst thing you can do is hit the snooze button on your alarm. This tells your subconscious that you don't want to start your day. It automatically makes you feel less excited.

Getting fresh air is another proven way to boost happiness. Get out of the house and office. Schedule time to be in nature. I recommend at least twenty minutes a day outdoors. It's proven that people who get that twenty minutes of sunshine are generally more positive. It also helps improve your memory.

Do you have a long, miserable commute to work? If it's wearing on your cheerfulness, try to make some changes. Overall, studies show that long commutes can affect your happiness levels. If you are the type of person who needs that alone time, maybe the long period of driving in solitude is right up your alley. If not, consider living closer to your job or asking to work from home a few days a week.

Aromatherapy can be helpful to some people. Essential oils like lavender are very calming. I swear, I went through a whole bottle of an essential oil called "past tense" when Shawn was out of town for six days and I was home alone with the kids. It was the week of a million drop-offs. Austin had football games far away at the same time as Daisy and Brody had home games in two different locations. It was also the start of the school year, and my daughter was a freshman. Her first class was at 5:30 a.m. I was getting up at 5:00 in the morning and going to bed at almost midnight. It was hell week for me. Not going to lie, I sat in the car and just cried, sniffing that oil a couple of times. Funny but not funny.

How about doing things you love? Listen to music that makes you feel good. Fun or uplifting music can lower anxiety, reduce pain, increase your immune system, and enhance positive emotions. The same goes for food. Eat the foods you love. Now, I'm not talking about stress eating or binging. I definitely want you to have a healthy relationship with food. Eat what you love to eat. For me, it's dark chocolate. My sweet indulgence. It's OK to have a little harmless, guilty pleasure. Actually, dark chocolate has several health benefits. There was a time I started to worry that I had a problem. I was locking my chocolate in the safe to hide it from the kids. I'd tiptoe off to my closet or the garage to secretly enjoy my beloved chocolate bar in peace. (I realize now it's not me who has the problem; it's those sneaky, gluttonous kids who have a problem.)

My point is, do things that bring you more happiness. It could be hot baths or soft jammies cuddled up on the couch in front of your favorite movie.

Focus on what you *can* do and not what you can't do. Focus on the future and find something to be excited about. Stop comparing yourself to others. This habit can be so damaging. It's such an easy thing to do. "She is further along than I am" or "I wish I had what he has." Especially because of social media being in our faces nonstop, we see post after post of people living their best life. We can fall into the trap of comparison. First off, most of those people are more messed up and unhappier than you. They just won't post about that part of their lives.

End negative thinking patterns. Stop listening to people or political news that makes you feel scared or angry. Unfollow people who rant and make you feel unhappy in any way. When thoughts enter your mind about what you don't have or how you are not good enough, focus on the good. Think instead about what is good right now in your life. I remember a time when I was so stressed out. It was back when I was going through the hardest part of my sickness. Business wasn't great, one of my kids was having difficulties at school, and my mom was also going through a tough time. It seemed like all roads led to stress. Nothing but negatives surrounded me. Every conversation and every phone call was nothing but drama or bad news. I sat down and forced myself to focus on the good. There was a lady who cleaned my house weekly who always did an amazing job. I wrote her name down first. I sure loved her during that whole mess. Next, I wrote down that my son, Austin, was happy and healthy. I continued this for about ten minutes until I had about fifteen lines written down and was ready to continue fighting my battles.

Please believe that you have the power to change your entire life. I hope you never stop striving for a better quality of life. I hope you will take risks and have no regrets. I hope when you reach your dreams, you don't stop— you set new goals. I hope you will dare to change the world in this short time you are here. I hope that *you* are your kids' hero and that you are the one who changes your family's legacy. I know you can. God has given you special and unique gifts and talents. He wants you to be happy, fulfilled, and lift up others.

Please believe that you have the power to change your entire life.

When things get hard, and they will, remember that is all part of the plan. Remember, adversity is for thy good. Take a rest when you need to, but just don't quit. Even if you have tried and tried to succeed and have not seen the fruits of your labor, don't give up. I have felt the embarrassment of failure. I know exactly how it feels when you think you have done all you can do and it still hasn't worked. I've wanted to quit a thousand times. I'm so grateful now that I didn't. I have seen hundreds of people who have failed over and over but went on to become incredible success stories. Hope is never lost. A boxer can get knocked down thirty-six times.

If he gets back up thirty-five times, he has lost. But if he gets back up thirty-six times, he still has a chance at becoming a champion. Just keep fighting. Clarity is your best friend; get clear on what you want, and I promise you already have everything inside you to make it happen.

ACTION STEP

Make a list of things that bring you joy. What is fun or comforting for you? Also, list people and things you are grateful for right now.

Last, focus on the good in your life. What are good things happening right now? What are you doing well? What are you most proud of? What and whom do you love? Who loves you? What is something you are looking forward to?

_____

_____

_____

_____

_____

_____

_____

_____

I feel so overwhelmed with gratitude. When I think of all the people who believed in me and helped me along this journey, my heart is so full. I appreciate the old version of myself for never giving up. I'm especially grateful for my husband, Shawn. He is the greatest partner I could ever ask for. I'm grateful for my family, my business, my team, my good times and my hard times, and I am grateful for you. Thank you for believing in me, and just know that I do believe in you.

ACKNOWLEDGMENTS

I want to recognize all the wonderful people who have contributed and added value to my life.

First, I want to thank my incredible team. They are my family and my strength. Team Revolution is a leadership team filled with caring individuals who want to change the world. People like Dana and Frank, Michael and Heather, Ericka, Wes, Kash, Rusty and Bridgett, Jazmin, Hanna, Adam and Johanna, Israel and Mary, Mauricio, Christina, Olivia and Tracy, and so many more who have been loyal friends and amazing wingmen and wingwomen. Also, to the thousands of other teammates who have believed in me and in our cause to serve others, I am so grateful to have you in my life. You inspire me to be better every day. The hard work and sacrifices I see you make and the challenges we have overcome together have built me into the leader I am today.

I'm so grateful for my amazing friend, Grace Suizo. She is always there to help with anything I need. She spent countless hours editing this book. This project was seamless and fun because of her contributions.

ACKNOWLEDGMENTS

I'm so grateful for my parents. I would not have become the woman I am without them. From my work ethic and tenacity to my independence and the dreams in my heart, my parents are the ones who put all those things in me. We have been through a lot, and they have taught me so much. I wouldn't change any of it. I love you.

I have been extremely blessed to have the most unbelievable mentors. Some people are lucky to have one great influential person in their life who cares about them, who inspires and challenges them. I have had several. John Shin coached me to think bigger. Jeff Levitan influenced my ability to lead, encouraged me, and showed me that I could win. Ed Mylett transferred not only skill but also belief as he challenged me and pulled me up when I was down. Monte Holm taught me to be mentally tough, and through his example, I learned how to be a compassionate leader. Rich and Cindy Thawley stretched my vision and believed in me. They cared about my family, my marriage, my spiritual growth, and my peace of mind. They gave me a role model of what I wanted my life to look like. They taught me how to be Happy & Strong. I can't express enough how incredibly humbled and grateful I feel to have the privilege to work with all of these outstanding human beings.

People ask me all the time, "Jaime, how do you do it all?" To be honest, I don't. I always have a support team. Neil Sandoval has been my right hand for so long. I really don't know how I would do it without him. He has filled many roles in my company and has even helped out with my kids at times. But most of all, he has been a sounding board and loyal friend. I appreciate him more than he knows.

I'm grateful for my younger siblings: Jessica, Danica, Melissa, Tessa, and David. You have no idea how much you have impacted my success and my life. You have been the reason I always kept going. It doesn't matter where we came from. All that matters is where we want to go! I love you so much. I'm so proud of you. Thank you, Jesi, for always being patient with me and for being my *why*!

To my babies: Daisy, Austin, Brody, and Benny. You are my new *whys*. Everything I do is for you. You are my heart and my joy. You will change the world.

And last, but certainly most important, thank you to my husband, Shawn. I'm grateful for your insatiable positive, optimistic attitude. We would never be where we are if it wasn't for your belief in us. Thank you for all your hard work and your incredible patience. Thank you for inspiring me, standing by me, pushing me, and loving me through it all. We have built this unbelievable life together. You are my Happy & Strong.